New Standards-Based Lessons for the Busy Elementary School Librarian

New Standards-Based Lessons for the Busy Elementary School Librarian

Social Studies

Joyce Keeling

LIBRARIES
UNLIMITED®

An Imprint of ABC-CLIO, LLC

Santa Barbara, California • Denver, Colorado

Library of Congress Cataloging-in-Publication Data

Names: Keeling, Joyce, author.
Title: New standards-based lessons for the busy elementary school librarian: social studies / Joyce Keeling.
Description: Santa Barbara, California : Libraries Unlimited, [2020] | Includes bibliographical references and index. |
Identifiers: LCCN 2019046382 (print) | LCCN 2019046383 (ebook) | ISBN 9781440872242 (paperback ; acid-free paper) | ISBN 9781440872259 (ebook)
Subjects: LCSH: Elementary school libraries—Standards—United States. | Information literacy—Study and teaching (Elementary)—United States. | Information literacy—Standards—United States. | Social sciences—Study and teaching (Elementary)—United States. | School librarian participation in curriculum planning—United States. | Education, Elementary—Curricula—United States.
Classification: LCC Z675.S3 K428 2020 (print) | LCC Z675.S3 (ebook) | DDC 027.8–dc23
LC record available at https://lccn.loc.gov/2019046382
LC ebook record available at https://lccn.loc.gov/2019046383

ISBN: 978–1–4408–7224–2 (paperback)
        978–1–4408–7225–9 (ebook)

24 23 22 21 20   1 2 3 4 5

This book is also available as an eBook.

Libraries Unlimited
An Imprint of ABC-CLIO, LLC

ABC-CLIO, LLC
147 Castilian Drive
Santa Barbara, California 93117
www.abc-clio.com

This book is printed on acid-free paper. ∞
Manufactured in the United States of America

Contents

Introduction

Teachers open up the world of knowledge and prepare students for their future. Teacher librarians "prepare students to live and learn in a world of information" (California Department of Education 2018). All students, including elementary students, must be able to question, access, interpret, and apply reliable sources to solve problems. Likewise, social studies students use inquiry, use data collection, and become problem solvers (National Curriculum for the Social Studies n.d.). Teacher librarians together with social studies teachers prepare students for the ever-changing global world using informed decisions from research and more as guided by standards.

According to Kelly (2017), standards have shown an important place in education since the 1980s and will continue to have a place in learning. One reason is that standards hold instructors and their schools accountable for learning quality and for student readiness. Standards set clear goals that can be measured, as well as show instructors the necessary outcomes.

Finally, standards provide a measurement for assessments. Instructors like the teacher librarian, social studies teachers, and others will show improved teaching outcomes from carefully defined standards-based learning. From carefully defined teaching comes successful student learning. Teachers give the instrumental instruction and direction, while the standards support the teachers.

Since both library and social studies teachers prepare students for the ever-changing world of global information, it is important to know how standards prepare students for learning and prepare teachers to feel comfortable with the standards. The standards used in this book are the American Association of School Librarians (AASL) Standards Framework for Learners, Common Core English Language Literacy State Standards, and the Social Studies Standards C3 (College, Career, and Civic Life) Framework. The AASL Standards Framework for Learners focuses on higher-level learning in an ever-changing world of print and digital resources (AASL 2017). It also stresses six key areas where students inquire, include, collaborate, curate, explore, and engage, as students use the domains of thinking, creating, sharing, and growing (Elementary Library). Teacher librarians base learning on the AASL Standards Framework for Learners and the Common Core and also connect those standards with other teachers' standards to create an even stronger base for teaching and student learning.

Teachers must collaborate for instruction using the standards in an effort to help make informed and accurate decisions. Standards sometimes connect with other standards, making teaching collaboration essential.

The four dimensions for the Social Studies C3 (College, Career, and Civic Life) Standards include students creating questions, applying social studies disciplinary cores, evaluating and using evidence, communicating, and taking action (National Council for Social Studies 2013), which is similar to the Common Core English Language Literacy State Standards. The Common Core English Language Literacy State Standards also advocate students questioning, planning, using tools, evaluating, and communicating (National Council for Social Studies 2013). The AASL Standards Framework for Learners, Common Core State Standards (CCSS), and Social Studies Standards C3 Framework share similar standards-based learning, which creates a bond of student learning and thus creates a perfect blend for collaborative instruction.

Some of the AASL Standards Framework for Learners (2019) advocate that students question (inquire), include and collaborate with others, curate and explore, use evidence, and solve problems in an ethical, engaging way. Access to current reliable information that is written for the student's interest and abilities makes for both excited and accurate learning. Moreover, both Social Studies and School Librarians Standards Frameworks focus on students using questions and accurate information and evidence to solve problems or take action.

Teacher librarians help students find current, accurate, and reliable information in print books and in digital formats. Teacher librarians locate the best information for the learning needs, abilities, grade levels, and interests for all students and classrooms. Social studies teachers know their students and work to find information to fit their students' needs as well. The results of teachers collaborating together produce higher success rate in student learning. Studies prove that teacher librarians working with others increases test scores and achievement (Library Research Service 2013; Starr 2010).

When all teachers are afforded the wealth of library resources and quality-tested online sources for an educational program with a qualified teacher librarian, student learning is increased. The teacher librarians first base their lessons on the librarian standards benchmark and on other subject standards that are being taught, connected to the Common Core Standards or to other such standards, and then collaborate and locate accurate library resources for lessons.

The Common Core English Language Art and Literacy, AASL Standards Framework for Learners, and other such standards provide the foundation for quality library and information skills instruction, providing a true connection between standards and instruction. Information literacy learning prepares students for college, career, and life readiness. The library standards framework and the social studies framework prepare learners for their futures (Social Studies Standards C3 Framework) and "shares the responsibility for literacy education" (National Council for the Social Studies 2013).

The chapters in this book are civics, economics, geography, and finally history. Chapter 1 covers topics of civics or civic principles from the Social Studies Standards C3 Framework, along with matching with English Language Arts Literacy Standards from the Common Core and the AASL Standards Framework for Learners. Civics means learning and applying responsible and effective citizenship skills. Using the Social Studies Standards, elementary students learn to be ready to be good citizens now and in their future.

According to the National Council for the Social Studies (2013), civics includes equality, liberty, freedom, trust, respect, cooperation, and the application of those actions for students for now and for their futures. Library information instruction also includes trust and respect, using resources, and cooperation and application of present and future student learning. Library instruction and resources ethically match civic and other social studies topics with all other academic needs matching accurate print and digital resources in the preparation for current and future student learning needs.

The second chapter is economics. Economics means understanding how to make good decisions when using limited resources. It involves costs, benefits, goods, services, needs, wants, and the global market. Chapter 2 discusses how people should ethically use resources, as required by the Social Studies Standards while matching language arts standards with the library information standards learner's framework.

The geography discipline is represented in the third chapter. Geography means using spatial outlooks of the earth, its people, and more. Chapter 3 includes geography topics such as making maps, other spatial locations, and more. The lessons are connected to student lives for student's effective problem solving needs involving questioning, ethical researching, evaluating, carefully answering questions for now and the future, which is also reflected in the library learner's standards framework.

The final chapter in this book is history as it can be taught with the three sets of standards. History studies historical ideas, beliefs, actions, and people, using relevant and current information. History is covered by looking at the past with perspectives, understanding, and application. The teacher librarian locates accurate sources and then will collaborate in instruction with the social studies teacher.

The 2017 AASL Standards Framework is an AASL Standards Framework for Learners. That framework involves inquire (question, seek knowledge, and use the evidence to inquire new knowledge); include (demonstrate inclusiveness and other points of view and work with others); collaborate (collaborate and learn from others); curate (get information from a carefully chosen variety of courses, question, organize, and create meaning); explore (grow from reflections and answering questions); and engage (safe and ethical caring and knowledge sharing) for the learners (AASL 2017). The lessons are written for the learners. Likewise, the AASL Standards Framework for Learners show the domain competencies of student learning or simply put learning categories for students to think (cognitive), create (psychomotor), share (affective), and grow (developmental personal growth) (AASL 2017). Students think, create, share, and grow through carefully orchestrated lessons based on the library standards framework from the qualified school librarian.

The AASL Standards Framework for Learners frames the standards for students to carefully inquire and seek knowledge, include others and other points of view, collaborate and learn from others, curate or get information, explore growth, and then engage or share learning. The teacher librarian shows students how to question or inquire, research ethically and use quality sources, process information carefully, and provide action. The teacher librarian helps social studies and all teachers by connecting teachers and students to quality materials in an ever-changing knowledge world of print resources and online resources, which is so important with the new standards (Parrott and Keith 2015).

The teacher librarian not only teaches their information literacy classes but also collaborates with other teachers, all based on learning standards. The teacher librarian not only directs libraries and the library holdings and teaches information literacy and language arts skills but also has three other roles. The teacher librarian serves as curriculum leader since he or she understands the school's standards, serves as information specialists for access to efficient and quality resources, and then serves as information service managers for meeting the needs for students and the classrooms (Angel and Morrison 2019). The teacher librarian provides resource services to help all other teachers and also collaborates in learning and teaching, leading the way through and to standards-based learning.

Likewise, the dedicated social studies teacher provides a wealth of social studies student learning that helps students to develop compelling and supportive type questions into purposeful inquiry while applying the social studies disciplines of civics, economics, geography, and history. The teacher guides student-planned learning from quality resources that fit the needs of the standards-based lesson and the needs of the students. The quality resources then help students develop a deep understanding requiring critical thinking. The social studies teacher helps students to be civic minded and be ready for their future careers and for college (C3). Collaborated teaching is beneficial for the social studies and all teachers.

Goddard and Goddard (2007) state that elementary school teacher collaboration may have increased student learning and will show less student behavioral issues and less intervention needs. When teachers collaborate, they share various instructional experiences, share expertise in their subject areas, and create a wealth of combined knowledge. Collaboration helps teachers increase their knowledge of teaching methods as well. Sullivan (2019) shows that a teacher librarian has access and the knowledge to collect sources to fit the learning needs and grade levels of students and can create that learning link through those resources, as well as through teaching the standards.

The qualified teacher librarian is an instrumental part of the school's learning community by providing access to current information and quality technology linked to the real world. The qualified teacher librarian not only provides access to quality-relevant print and digital resources but also links learning to those resources and promotes reading. The AASL (2017) states, "Qualified school librarians have been educated and certified to perform interlinked, interdisciplinary, and cross-cutting roles as instructional leaders [and more]." The teacher librarian with carefully chosen resources prepares learners for "college, career, and life" (AASL 2017).

The Social Studies C3 Standards are college, career, and (civic) life as well, which is formulated by the dedicated social studies teacher. The basis for learning is that all teaching is first set on the solid foundation of a standards foundation. Well-written and orchestrated standards like the CS standards and others can not only help to aid in learning but also helps students become active learners (National Council for the Social Studies: Preparing Students for College, Career, and Civic Life).

"The C3 Social Studies Framework and the AASL or American Association of School Librarians Standards [Framework for Learners] mention learning for the future, and emphasizes inquiry in learning and open doors for social studies teachers and librarians and others to collaborate." The Social Studies Framework frames rigorous learning for current learning and to prepare student learning for student futures. The AASL Standards Framework for Learners also frames learning and provides rigorous learning from research as students inquire, include, collaborate, curate, explore, and then engage. Both C3 and AASL Standards Learners Framework create a solid foundation for learning and teacher instruction, as each set of standards is merged into learning in the school library and classrooms.

The Common Core English Language Arts and Literacy educational standards ensure that students will be ready for college and careers (Iowa Department of Education 2018) through literacy instruction. The CCSS have been adopted by forty-two states and four territories and are "informed by other top-top performing countries" (CCSS 2019). Common Core Language Arts and Literacy can be seen in the elementary library curriculum, as everything taught in the library curriculum can be matched with Common Core Language Arts and Literacy too. A teacher librarian helps other instructors follow the CCSS (and Social Studies Standards and more) through providing helpful library resources as well as insight into the standards. The CCSS give clear, consistent learning guidelines and are a way to measure student progress (CCSS Initiative 2019).

The CCSS or Common Core State Standards involve critical problem solving skills, as does the Social Studies and National School Library Standards Framework for Learners as well. Furthermore, the CCSS ensure that students are indeed ready for current and future success, which is also seen in the AASL Standards Framework for Learners and the Social Standards Framework. With the combination of three different sets of standards that agree in many ways including the provision of clear and consistent learning guidelines, future growth, and so much more, students will indeed be ready for the futures and find success in problem solving skills.

Library instruction with social studies and many other subject areas are based on inquiry learning with twenty-first century learning standards as students think, create, share, and grow through carefully planned lessons and through quality resources, as all set to standards. This book approaches the AASL standards for the learners. There are also the teacher librarian standards that are naturally mingled with the AASL standards for learners. The teacher librarian standards suggest that students be able to think critically, work alone and with others, collaborate, gather meaning from various print and digital information resources, feel technology encouragement, increase curiosity, feel encouraged to read in a champion way, and then want to keep learning for life and more (Iowa Department of Education 2019).

Those teacher librarian standards are naturally compatible with the AASL standards for learners, since both suggest that students collaborate and gather meaning, using various print and digital resources. If students have a qualified teacher librarian, they will surely want to keep learning and reading for life. The teaching standards "represent a set of knowledge, skills and dispositions that reflects the best evidence available regarding quality standards" (Iowa Department of Education 2018). All instructions in this book are set on clearly defined learner standards and provide clearly given instructions.

Since the C3 Social Studies Framework or College, Career, and Civic Life Framework for Social Studies Standards is set up from kindergarten through second grades and then from third to fifth grades (National Council for the Social Studies 2013), this book is organized in that same way. Each chapter's subsections split each chapter into kindergarten through second grades and then third through fifth grades. The lessons in this book can be altered in themselves, fit to another grade, or can have standards changed around or added, as social studies topics must be applied to each U.S. state, territory, or other such needs.

However, there is no room to include all social studies topics. This author must explain that it is difficult to keep up with ever-changing history, social studies subjects, and other core subjects that change with the changing world, which is evident in the difficulty of finding all current sources. All print book and online (digital) resources in this book are evaluated for efficient learning for topics in this book. Each interactive and thus engaging student lesson is formatted to last for about twenty minutes. Most of this book's lessons are collaborative student-type lessons so that no learners are left behind.

All of the book's suggested sources have been evaluated and matched to the AASL Standards Framework for Learners, Common Core English Language Arts and Literacy, and the Social Studies C3 Framework. The standards provide consistent learning and teaching guidelines. Teachers provide the learning methods. Collaborated teaching, standards, and student learning provide the maximum of student achievement for current and future student learning.

References

American Association of School Librarians (AASL). "AASL Standards Framework for Learners." Updated 2017. https://standards.aasl.org/framework/.

American Association of School Librarians (AASL). "Common Beliefs." Updated 2017. https://standards.aasl.org/beliefs/.

Angel, Kathryn N., and Valerie Morrison. "21st Century Librarians and Computer Teachers. Updated Australian School Library Association. What Is a Teacher Librarian?" Updated 2019. http://www.asla.org.au/advocacy/what-is-a-teacher-librarian.aspx.

California Department of Education. "School Libraries." Updated 2018. https://www.cde.ca.gov/ci/cr/cf/cefschoollibraries.asp.

Common Core State Standards (CCSS) Initiative. "What Parents Should Know." Updated 2019. http://www.corestandards.org/what-parents-should-know/.

Goddard, Yvonne L., and Roger D. Goddard. 2007. "A Theoretical and Empirical Investigation of Teacher Collaboration for School Improvement and Student Achievement in Public Elementary Schools." *Teachers College Record* 109: 877–896.

Iowa Department of Education. "Explore the Common Core: Literacy." https://iowacore.gov/iowa-core/subject/literacy.

Iowa Department of Education. "Iowa Teaching Standards and Criteria." Updated 2019. https://educateiowa.gov/pk-12/educator-quality/teacher-quality#iowa_Teaching_Standards_and_Criteria.

Iowa Department of Education. "Vision for Iowa's School Libraries." Updated 2019. https://educateiowa.gov/pk-12/instruction/school-library.

Kelly, Denise. "3 Reasons Standards Are Essential to Educational Success." Updated 2017. https://www.apexlearning.com/blog/3-reasons-standards-are-essential-to-educational-success.

Library Research Service. "School Libraries & Student Achievement." Updated 2013. https://www.lrs.org/documents/school/school_library_impact.jpg.

National Council for the Social Studies. "C3 Framework for Social Studies." Updated 2013. https://www.socialstudies.org/sites/default/files/c3/C3-Framework-for-Social-Studies .pdf.

National Council for the Social Studies: Preparing Students for College, Career, and Civic Life. "National Curriculum Standards for Social Studies: Introduction." https://www .socialstudies.org/standards/introduction.

National Curriculum for the Social Studies. n.d. "National Curriculum Standards for Social Studies." https://www.socialstudies.org/standards/introduction.

Parrott, Deborah J., and Keith, Karen J. "Three Heads Are Better Than One." *Teacher Librarian*. Updated 2015. https://www.researchgate.net/publication/280090008_Parrott_D_J_ Keith_K_J_2015_Three_Heads_Are_Better_Than_One_Teacher_Librarian_425_12- 18.

Starr, Linda. "Strong Libraries Improve Student Learning." Education World. Updated 2010. https://www.educationworld.com/a_admin/admin/admin178.shtml.

Sullivan, Kerri. 2018. "Librarian Teacher Collaboration: Creating a Culture of Learning." *Collected Magazine* 10+.

Standards

There are three sets of standards for this book: the American Association of School Librarians Standards for Learners, Social Studies Standards—the Inquiry Arc of the C3 (College, Career, and Civic Life) Framework, and the Common Core English Language Arts Literacy Standards (CCSS).

The American Association of School Librarians (AASL) Standards Framework for Learners

AASL Standards for Learners are listed at the start of each chapter, as each of those given standards are used in each lesson, as they are centered on students who "inquire, include, collaborate, curate, explore, and engage." American Association of School Librarians. "AASL Standards Framework for Learners." Updated 2017. https://standards.aasl.org/framework.

The AASL Standards Framework for Learners is seen at the start of each chapter, as each lesson adheres to what is given here.

The AASL Standards Framework for Learners encourages learners to

1. Inquire through such means as questioning, using evidence, connecting to prior knowledge, making decisions, and more.
2. Include through such means as discussing, examining other's views, reflecting, and more.
3. Collaborate through participating, obtaining feedback, solving problems with others to connect shared learning, and more.
4. Curate through such means as determining a need and then gathering and organizing information from a variety of accurate resources, reflecting, and more.
5. Explore through such means as reading, writing, creating, asking questions, solving problems, expressing being curious, reflecting, and more.
6. Engage through such means as applying and evaluating information and sources to learning in an ethical way, including avoiding plagiarism and more.

Excerpted and adapted from *National School Library Standards for Learners, School Librarians, and School Libraries* by the American Association of School Librarians, a division of the American Library Association, copyright © 2018 American Library Association. Available for download at www.standards.aasl.org. Used with permission.

American Association of School Librarians. *AASL Standards Framework for Learners.* Chicago, IL: American Library Association, 2017.

Social Studies Standards—the Inquiry Arc of the C3 (College, Career, and Civic Life) Framework

Social Studies Standards—the Inquiry Arc of the C3 (College, Career, and Civic Life) Framework is listed by each disciplinary subject for each matching social studies chapter.

Civics (Chapter 1)

Civics K-2
D2.Civ.l.K-2. Describe the roles and responsibilities of people in authority.
D2.Civ.2.K-2. Describe how all people have roles in a community.
D2.Civ.3.K-2 Describe the need for rules in and out of school.
D.2.Civ.10.K-2. Compare own point of view with others.

Civics 3-5
D2.Civ.1.3-5. Know responsibilities and powers of government officials.
D2.Civ.2.3-5. Describe how a democracy relies on people to participate.
D2.Civ.5.3-5. Look at the origin and purpose of rules, laws, and the U.S. Constitution.
D2.Civ.10.3-5. Identify beliefs, experiences, outlook, and values of own and others views on civic issues.

Economics (Chapter 2)

Economics K-2
D2.Eco.1.K-2. Explain how scarcity makes decisions.
D2.Eco.2.K-2. Know the benefits and cost of personal decisions.
D2.Eco.4.K-2. Describe goods and services of local community people.
D2.Eco.6.K-2. Explain how people earn money.
D2.Eco.9.K-2 Explain the role of banks.
D2.Eco.10.K-2. Explain saving.

Economics 3-5
D2.Eco.1.3-5. Know the positive and negative costs of choices.
D2.Eco.3.3-5. Identify variety of resources like human capital, physical capital, and natural resources to make goods and services.
D2.Eco.10.3-5. Explain interest rates.
D2.Eco.12.3-5. Explain the ways that government pays for the goods and services it gives.
D2.Eco.14.K-2. Describe why people trade goods and services with other countries.

Geography (Chapter 3)

Geography K-2
D2.Geo.3.K-2. Use maps, globes, and other such geographic models to identify cultural and environmental places.

D2.Geo.4.K-2. Discuss the effects of weather, climate, and other such things that affect lives in a place.

D2.Geo.1.3-5. Create maps and other graphical representations of both known and unknown places.

Geography 3-5

D2.Geo.1.3-5. Create maps and other graphical representations of both known and unknown places.

D2.Geo.2.3-5. Use maps and other images to show the relationship of places and regions and their environment.

D2.Geo.4.3-5. Describe how culture influences the way people change and adapt to their environments.

D2.Geo.8.3-5. Describe how human settlements and movements connect to location and natural resources.

History (Chapter 4)

History K-2

D2.His.2.K-2. Compare life in the past to the present.

D2.His.3.K-2. Create questions on individuals and groups who made an important historical change.

D2.His.16.K-2. Select the reasons that explain a historical event or development.

History 3-5

D2.His.2.3-5. Compare life in certain historical times to life today.

D2.His.3.3-5. Create questions on individuals and groups who made historical changes.

D2.His.16.3-5. Use evidence to create a claim about the past.

National Council for the Social Studies. *Social Studies for the Next Generation: Purposes, Practices, and Implications of the College, Career, and Civic Life (C3) Framework for Social Studies State Standards.* Silver Spring, MD. 2013.

Common Core English Language Arts Literacy Standards (CCSS)

Kindergarten

Kindergarten Common Core (Literacy)—Reading Literature

CCSS.ELA-Literacy.RL.K.1

• With prompting and support, ask and answer questions about key details in a text.

CCSS.ELA-Literacy.RL.K.3

• With prompting and support, identify characters, settings, and major events in a story, using key details.

CCSS.ELA-Literacy.RL.K.6

• With prompting and support, name the author and illustrator of a story and define the role of each in telling the story.

CCSS.ELA-Literacy.RL.K.7

• With prompting and support, describe the relationship between illustrations and the story in which they appear (e.g., what moment in a story an illustration depicts).

Kindergarten Common Core (Literacy)—Reading Informational Texts

CCSS.ELA-Literacy.RI.K.2

• With prompting and support, identify the main topic and retell key details of a text.

First Grade

First Grade Common Core (Literacy)—Reading Literature

CCSS.ELA-Literacy.RL.1.1
• Ask and answer questions about key details in a text.

CCSS.ELA-Literacy.RL.1.3
• Describe characters, settings, and major events in a story, using key details.

First Grade Common Core (Literacy)—Reading Informational Texts

CCSS.ELA-Literacy.RL.1.5
• Explain major differences between books that tell stories and books that give information, drawing on a wide reading of a range of text types. (This is applied to other grades as well.)

CCSS.ELA-Literacy.RL.1.7
• Use illustrations and details in a story to describe its characters, settings, or events.

Second Grade

Second Grade Common Core (Literacy)—Reading Literature

CCSS.ELA-Literacy.RL.2.1
• Ask and answer such questions as *who, what, where, when, why*, and *how* to demonstrate understanding of key details in a text.

CCSS.ELA-Literacy.RL.2.7
• Use the information gained from the illustrations and words in a print or digital text to demonstrate understanding of its characters, setting, or plot.

Second Grade Common Core (Literacy)—Reading Informational Texts

CCSS.ELA-Literacy.RI.2.1
• Ask and answer such questions as who, what, where, when, why, and how to demonstrate understanding of the key details in a text.

CCSS.ELA-Literacy.RI.2.6
• Identify the main purpose of a text, including what the author wants to answer, explain, or describe.

Third Grade

Third Grade Common Core (Literacy)—Reading Literature

CCSS.ELA-Literacy.RL.3.1
• Ask and answer questions to demonstrate understanding of a text, referring explicitly to the text as the basis for the answers.

CCSS.ELA-Literacy.RL.3.3
• Describe characters in a story (e.g., their traits, motivations, or feelings), and explain how their actions contribute to the sequence of events.

CCSS.ELA-Literacy.RL.3.5
• Refer to parts of stories, dramas, and poems, when writing or speaking about a text; using terms such a *chapter, scene*, and *stanza*, describe how each successive part builds on earlier sections.

Third Grade Common Core (Literacy)—Reading Informational Texts

CCSS.ElA-Literacy.RI.3.1
- Ask and answer questions to demonstrate understanding of a text, referring explicitly to the text for answers.

CCSS.ELA-Literacy.RI.3.7
- Use the information gained from illustrations (e.g., maps and photographs) and the words in a text to demonstrate understanding of the text (e.g., where, when, why, and how key events occur).

Fourth Grade

Fourth Grade Common Core (Literacy)—Reading Literature

CCSS.ELA-Literacy.RL.4.1
- Refer to details and examples in a text when explaining what the text says explicitly and when drawing inferences from the text.

CCSS.ELA.RL.4.2
- Determine a theme of a story, drama, or poem from details in the text; summarize the text.

CCSS.ELA.RL.4.9
- Describe in depth a character, a setting, or an event in a story or drama, drawing on specific details in the text (e.g., a character's thoughts, words, or actions).

Fourth Grade Common Core (Literacy)—Reading Informational Texts

CCSS.ELA-Literacy.RI.4.1
- Refer to details and examples in a text when explaining what the text says explicitly and when drawing inferences from the text.

CCSS.ELA-Literacy.RI.4.7
- Interpret the information presented visually, orally, or quantitatively (e.g., in charts, graphs, diagrams, timelines, animations, or interactive elements on web pages), and explain how the information contributes to an understanding of the text in which it appears.

Fifth Grade

Fifth Grade Common Core (Literacy)—Reading Literature

CCSS.ELA-Literacy.RL.5.2
- Determine a theme of a story, drama, or poem from details in the text, including how characters in a story or drama respond to challenges or how the speaker in a poem reflects upon a topic; summarize the text.

CCSS.ELA.RL.5.3
- Compare and contrast two or more characters, setting, or events in a story or drama, drawing on specific details in a text (e.g., how characters interact).

Fifth Grade Common Core (Literacy)—Reading Informational Texts

CCSS.ELA-Literacy.RI.5.7
- Draw on the information from multiple print or digital sources, demonstrating the ability to locate an answer to a question quickly or to solve a problem efficiently.

CCSS.ELA-Literacy.R.I.5.9
- Integrate the information from several texts on the same topic in order to write or speak about the subject knowledgeably.

Governors Association Center for Best Practices and Council of Chief State School Officers (2010). *Common Core State Standards (Literacy)*. Washington, DC: National Governors Association Center for Best Practices and Council of Chief State School Officers. http://www.corestandards.org/.

Educators may prefer to intermingle other or additional standards or simply select some or all of the given standards. Each lesson holds a wealth of resources for educators to pick and choose from to support the standards-based learning and subsequently lessons. The standards are the foundation or framework of learning, but the teachers hold the key.

Chapter 1

The School Librarian and Social Studies Teachers with Civics

This chapter covers the topics of civics or civic principles as stated in the Social Studies Standards and how to become a responsible and an effective citizen. It also covers library literacy standards and language arts standards. The teacher librarians partner with the elementary social studies teachers to provide excellence in education with engaging lessons, with library and online resources as students collaborate with each other in order to create learning for all. Lessons are approximately twenty minutes long.

If not using some of those standards, the educator will apply other standards. Likewise, the educator can pick and choose any of the three sets of standards or use all of those standards in each lesson. The mixture of social studies, language arts/literacy, and library or literacy skills and resources provides well-rounded opportunities for successful learning.

This chapter begins with lessons for kindergarten, with those lessons being usable for other lower elementary grades, and then the lessons move upward to the fifth grade. Grade levels are not narrowly assigned per lesson but are suggested. Furthermore, this book not only engages all learners but also offers lessons that can be intermingled for other elementary grades. There are many resources that have been tested before being suggested with each lesson, offering more teaching opportunities. However, the main focus is student-engaged learning—educators teaching through helpful plans and resources, all based on standards.

Standards

AASL Standards Framework for Learners

AASL Standards for Learners are listed at the start of each chapter, as each of those given standards are used in each lesson, as they are centered on students who "inquire, include, collaborate, curate, explore, and engage." American Association of School Librarians. "AASL Standards Framework for Learners." Updated 2017. https://standards.aasl.org/framework/.

AASL Standards Framework for Learners encourage learners to

1. Inquire through such means as questioning, using evidence, connecting to prior knowledge, making decisions, and more.
2. Include through such means as discussing, examining other's views, reflecting, and more.
3. Collaborate through participating, obtaining feedback, solving problems with others to connect shared learning, and more.
4. Curate through such means as determining a need and then gathering and organizing information from a variety of accurate resources, reflecting, and more.
5. Explore through such means as reading, writing, creating, asking questions, solving problems, expressing being curious, reflecting, and more.
6. Engage through such means as applying and evaluating information and sources to learning in an ethical way, including avoiding plagiarism and more.

Excerpted and adapted from *National School Library Standards for Learners, School Librarians, and School Libraries* by the American Association of School Librarians, a division of the American Library Association, copyright © 2018 American Library Association. Available for download at https://standards.aasl.org/framework. Used with permission.

Social Studies Standards—the Inquiry Arc of the C3 (College, Career, and Civic Life) Framework

Civics

Civics K-2
D2.Civ.l.K-2. Describe the roles and responsibilities of people in authority.
D2.Civ.2.K-2. Describe how all people have roles in a community.
D2.Civ.3.K-2. Describe the need for rules in and out of school.
D.2.Civ.10.K-2. Compare own point of view with others.

Civics 3-5
D2.Civ.1.3-5. Know responsibilities and powers of government officials.
D2.Civ.2.3-5. Describe how a democracy relies on people to participate.
D2.Civ.5.3-5. Look at the origin and purpose of rules, laws, and the U.S. Constitution.
D2.Civ.10.3-5. Identify beliefs, experiences, outlook, and values of own and others views on civic issues.

National Council for the Social Studies. *Social Studies for the Next Generation: Purposes, Practices, and Implications of the College, Career, and Civic Life (C3) Framework for Social Studies State Standards.* Silver Spring, MD. 2013.

Common Core Standards—Literacy

Common Course Language Arts Literacy Standards or CCSS, which are given in the introductory standards section of the book, are seen with each lesson. These standards are too lengthy to be given here at the start of each chapter, but they are seen as needed for each lesson. For a complete look at this book's Common Core Standards in Literacy, refer to the introduction section.

Educators may prefer to intermingle other or additional standards or simply select some or all of the given standards. Each lesson holds a wealth of resources for educators to pick and choose from to support the standards-based learning and subsequently lessons for successful student learning. The standards are the foundation or framework of learning, but the teachers hold the key.

Schools Rule!

It is fun at school, when rules are followed.
Are there some things you should not do at school?

Draw three school rules in the box.

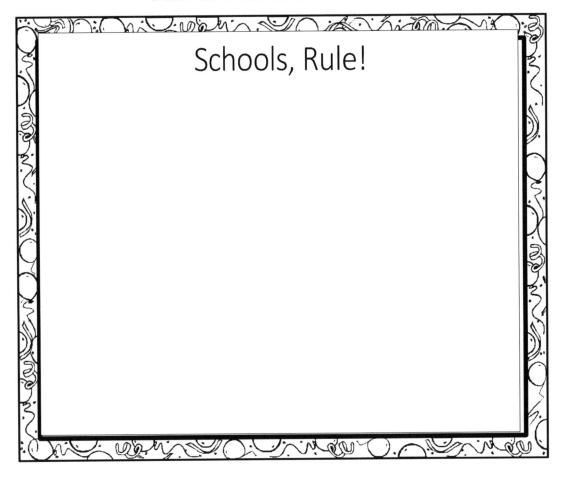

Schools, Rule!

Schools Rule, Directions

Civics: Rules
Grade Levels Suggested: Kindergarten or Kindergarten–Second Grades

Standards

AASL Standards

AASL Standards are listed at the start of each chapter, as each of those given standards are used in each lesson, as the lessons are centered on students who "inquire, include, collaborate, curate, explore, and engage" (American Association of School Librarians 2017)

Common Core Language Arts Literacy Standards

CCSS.ELA-Literacy.RL.K.3 • With prompting and support, identify characters, settings, and major events in a story, using key details.

CCSS.ELA-Literacy.RL.K.7 • With prompting and support, describe the relationship between illustrations and the story in which they appear (e.g., what moment in a story an illustration depicts).

CCSS.ELA-Literacy.RL.1.5 • Explain major differences between books that tell stories and books that give information, drawing on a wide reading of a range of text types.

Social Studies Standards C3

D2.Civ.3.K-2. Describe the need for rules in and out of school.

Learning Objectives

Students will

- Discuss and recognize the need for rules in school.
- Discuss and note the differences between nonfiction and fiction books.
- Discuss the author, title, and purpose of a fiction book on school rules.
- Gather and share information from nonfiction books about school rules.
- Illustrate three school rules.

Suggested Teaching Team

School library and social studies teachers.

Instructional Procedure

Lessons will be a collaborative lesson for most of the class time. Teachers are always checking for understanding. Students are more often than not involved in paired or team work so that all learners have a chance to gather ideas and be involved. Assessment is ongoing observation while also checking for understanding.

1. Teachers will read a humorous picture fiction book on not following rules at school. Class questions and discussions will cover the title, author, and theme. Students will inquire, collaborate, and explore school rules like being kind, following teacher rules, and so on, as all connected to prior knowledge.

2. Teachers will continue the discussion on rules in the school library and the classroom. From discussions, two to three rules in two- to three-worded statements will be posted.

3. Teachers will introduce nonfiction books on rules and laws. As guided by teachers, students will briefly explain the differences between nonfiction and fiction.

4. Student groups will then question and explore the illustrations in nonfiction books on rules in school, or rules in the gym, library, bus, playground, and more, in order to further explore school rules.

5. Engaged student groups will report back to the class to explain what school rules they found and how they solved their quest to find more rules. From student reporting, teachers will add two or three more rules to the list on rules in the school library and classroom.

6. Teachers will help students narrow down the list to only three or four rules.

7. Students will take action and illustrate three rules on their worksheet-framed box. Students will apply learning by coloring the frame and cutting out the worksheet box for a reminder to be posted on student desks.

Recommended Resources

Fiction

Booker, Dwayne. *Fiona Follows School Rules*. New York: Rosen, 2018.

Gill, Timothy, and Neil Numberman. *Flip & Fin: We Rule the School*. New York: Greenwillow, 2014.

LaFaye, A. *No Frogs in School*. New York: Sterling, 2018.

Parsley, Elisie. *If You Want to Bring an Alligator to School, Don't!* New York: Little, Brown Books, 2015.

Nonfiction

Bloom, Paul. *Rules in the Classroom*. Milwaukee, WI: Gareth Stevens, 2015.

Bloom, Paul. *School Rules Book Set*. Milwaukee, WI: Gareth Stevens, 2016.

Coan, Sharon. *Rules at School*. Huntington Beach, CA: Teacher Created Materials, 2016.

Harry Kindergarten Music. "The Rules of the Classroom." Video. Updated 2014. https://www.youtube.com/watch?v=uWXPCP8t00M.

Hely, Patrick. *Why Do We Have Rules in School?* New York: PowerKids, 2019.

Jeffries, Corina. *Following Rules at School: Understanding Citizenship*. New York: Rosen, 2018.

Mason, Helen. *Be an Active Citizen at Your School*. New York: Crabtree, 2017.

Troupe, Thomas K., and Rhea Zhai. *Schools Have Rules*. Mankato, MN: Picture Window Books, 2018.

Wonder Grove. "Understand the Basic School Rules." Video. [Sign Language Used]. Updated 2013. https://www.youtube.com/watch?v=RyLzsQKFpB0.

Firefighter or Police Officer

Draw what a police officer and a firefighter does.

A police officer helps like this:

A firefighter helps like this:

Honor police officers or firefighters. Wear a badge.

Firefighter or Police Officer, Directions

Civics: People in authority
Grade Levels Suggested: Kindergarten or Kindergarten–Second Grades

Standards

AASL Standards

AASL Standards are listed at the start of each chapter, as each of those given standards are used in each lesson, as the lessons are centered on students who "inquire, include, collaborate, curate, explore, and engage" (American Association of School Librarians 2017).

Common Core Language Arts Literacy Standards

CCSS.ELA-Literacy.RL.K.7 • With prompting and support, describe the relationship between illustrations and the story in which they appear (e.g., what moment in a story an illustration depicts).

CCSS.ELA-Literacy.RL.K.3 • With prompting and support, identify characters, settings, and major events in a story, using key details.

CCSS.ELA-Literacy.RI.K.2 • With prompting and support, identify the main topic and retell key details of a text.

CCSS.ELA-Literacy.RL.1.5 • Explain major differences between books that tell stories and books that give information, drawing on a wide reading of a range of text types.

Social Studies Standards C3

D2.Civ.l.K-2. Describe the roles and responsibilities of people in authority.

Learning Objectives

Students will

- Discuss and recognize the helpful roles of a firefighter and police officer in their community.
- Recognize the title, author, and major events of fiction books and the books' illustrations.
- Explore information on how firefighters and police officers help in a community using the key details of nonfiction books.
- Apply and draw how firefighters and police officers help in a community.
- Recognize the differences between fiction and nonfiction books.

Suggested Teaching Team

School library and social studies teachers.

Instructional Procedure

Lessons will be a collaborative lesson for most of the class time. Students are more often than not involved in paired or team work so that all learners have a chance to gather ideas and be involved. Assessment is ongoing observation while also checking for understanding.

1. Teachers will read and show a police officer and firefighter fiction picture book while discussing the authors, titles, and illustrations with students.
2. Teachers will lead a discussion on what police officers and firefighters do, according to students' prior knowledge and as sparked from the teacher-read fiction picture books.
3. Teachers will briefly show the cover of a nonfiction book. With prompting, students will explain the differences between fiction and nonfiction.

4. Student pairs will question or inquire, gather information, or curate as they examine key details through illustrations and explore firefighter and police officer nonfiction books.

5. Student pairs will explain what firefighters and police officers do to help in their community, as seen in the nonfiction books. From class explanations, teachers will post two to three ways that show how those officers help in the community.

6. On their worksheets, individual students will conclude and thus apply their knowledge on how firefighters and police officers help in their community, when students illustrate at least two different ways.

7. Students will color, cut out, and wear a badge of their choice.

Recommended Resources

Fiction

Dean, James. *Firefighter Pete*. New York: HarperFestival, 2018.

Elya, Susan M. *Fire! Fuego! Brave Bomberos*. New York: Bloomsbury, 2013.

Mammano, Julie. *Rhinos Who Rescue*. Concord, CA: Chronicle Books, 2007.

Meadows, Michelle. *Traffic Pups*. New York: Simon Schuster Books, 2011.

Scarry, Richard. *Richard Scarry's Smokey the Fireman*. New York: Random House, 2015.

Nonfiction

Bellisario, Gina. *Firefighters in My Community* (*Meet a Community Helper*). Minneapolis, MN: Lerner, 2019.

Bellisario, Gina. *Police Officers in My Community* (*Meet a Community Helper*). Minneapolis, MN: Lerner, 2019.

Bowman, Chris. *Firefighters*. Birmingham, AL: Bellwether Media, 2018.

Conway, Sommer. *My Aunt Is a Firefighter*. New York: Rosen, 2019.

Gaertner, Meg. *Police Officers* (*Community Workers-4D*). Minneapolis, MN: Pop!, 2019.

Huffman, Mindy. *I Want to Be a Police Officer*. New York: Rosen, 2019.

Kenan, Tessa. *Hooray for Firefighters*. Minneapolis, MN: Lerner, 2018.

Leaf, Christina. *Police Officers. Community Workers*. Birmingham, AL: Bellwether Media, 2018.

Parkes, Elle. *Hooray for Police Officers*. Minneapolis, MN: Lerner, 2017.

Ready, Dee. *Firefighters Help*. Minneapolis, MN: Capstone Press, 2013.

Ready, Dee. *Police Officers Help*. Minneapolis, MN: Capstone Press, 2014.

Rogers, Kate. *Police Officers on the Job*. San Diego, CA: KidHaven Publishing, 2017.

Royston, Angela. *Fire Fighter!* New York: DK, 2011.

Shepherd, Jodie. *A Day with Firefighters*. Chicago, IL: Children's Press, 2013.

Good Citizen

1. What is a good citizen?

2. What are ways to be a good citizen? Color the ways.

3. How will you be a good citizen? On the sign, draw being a good citizen.

Good Citizen, Directions

Civics: Citizenship at school and in their family's community
Grade Levels Suggested: First Grade or Kindergarten–Second Grades

Standards

AASL Standards

AASL Standards are listed at the start of each chapter, as each of those given standards are used in each lesson.

Common Core Language Arts Literacy Standards

CCSS.ELA-Literacy.RL.1.3 • Describe characters, settings, and major events in a story, using key details.
CCSS.ELA-Literacy.RL.1.5 • Explain major differences between books that tell stories and books that give information, drawing on a wide reading of a range of text types.
CCSS.ELA-Literacy.RL.1.7 • Use illustrations and details in a text to describe its key ideas.

Social Studies Standards C3

D2.Civ.2.K-2. Describe how all people have roles in a community.
D.2.Civ.10.K-2. Compare own point of view with others.

Learning Objectives

Students will

- Define the basic concepts of good citizenship at school and in their community.
- Explain the differences between nonfiction and fiction.
- Explain the characters, setting, and main event of a fiction book.
- Relate good citizenship to themselves in a worksheet.

Suggested Teaching Team

School library and social studies teachers.

Instructional Procedure

Lessons will be a collaborative lesson for most of the class time. Teachers are always checking for understanding. Students are more often than not involved in paired or team work so that all learners have a chance to gather ideas and be involved. Assessment is ongoing observation while also checking for understanding.

1. Teachers will briefly discuss that good citizenship would mean such things as being respectful and working to make their school and their community a better place.
2. Teachers will discuss the title and author of a fiction picture book on school or their family's community citizenship. The fiction book will be read and followed by a discussion of characters, setting, and main event or main plot. The book will be related to good citizenship. For instance, if reading a humorous book about the library, being a good citizen would be taking care of books and so on. Students will give their own points of view, as well as connecting to prior knowledge.
3. Before being given nonfiction books to research, students will recall the differences between nonfiction and fiction.

4. Student groups will be given nonfiction books on being a good citizen at their school or in their family's community. Students will develop problem solving skills by questioning and examining the illustrations and some of the words in order to find ways to be a good citizen. Students will discuss and give their findings to the class.

5. Those findings will be written in two to three worded sentences and displayed by the teachers. Teachers will also discuss and summarize what makes them a good citizen at school or with their home community, and write that definition in simple short sentences too.

6. When looking at the student worksheet, teachers will explain that being at school or in their community, a good citizen could be helping to plant flowers, following stop sign laws, or picking up litter. Students will conclude and take action by applying learning, by completing their worksheets about what is a good citizen, coloring ways to be a good citizen, and then drawing how they could be a good citizen either at school or in their community.

Recommended Resources

Fiction

Gassman, Julie. *Do Not Bring Your Dragon to the Library*. North Mankato, MN: Capstone, 2016.

Mora, Pat. *I Pledge Allegiance*. New York: Alfred A. Knopf, 2014.

Parsely, Elise. *If You Ever Want to Bring a Circus to the Library, Don't!* New York: Little, Brown Books, 2017.

Walton, Phillip. *Citizen Miles: A Lesson in Citizenship*. Edina, MN: Rising Star Studios, 2010.

Nonfiction

Bonwill, Ann. *We Are Good Citizens*. Chicago, IL: Children's Press, 2019.

Coan, Sharon. *Being a Good Citizen*. Huntington Beach, CA: Teacher Created Materials, 2016.

Hoffman, Mary A. *I Am a Good Citizen*. Milwaukee, WI: Gareth Stevens Publishers, 2011.

James, Emily. *How to Be a Good Citizen*. North Mankato, MN: Capstone Press, 2018.

Jeffries, Corina. *Citizenship at School: Understanding Citizenship*. New York: Rosen, 2018.

Kreisman, Rachelle. *Being a Good Citizen*. Concord, MA: Red Chair Press, 2016.

Pegis, Jessica. *What Is Citizenship?* North Mankato, MN: Capstone Press, 2016.

VanVoorst, Jenny F. *I Am a Good Citizen*. New York: Bellwether Media, 2019.

VanVoorst, Jenny F. *I Am a Good Citizen*. New York: Scholastic, 2019.

Everyone at School Helps

1. Everyone at school helps. Draw a line on how they help to the people.

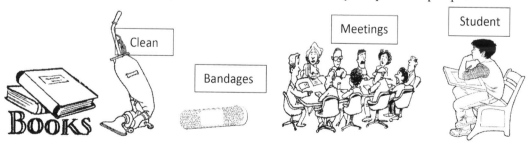

2. Draw yourself in the box at top of the school. How can you help too?

Everyone at School Helps, Directions

Civics: Authority school roles: Custodian, librarian, nurse, principal, and teacher
Grade Levels Suggested: First Grade or Kindergarten–Second Grades

Standards

AASL Standards are listed at the start of each chapter, as each of those given standards are used in each lesson, as they are centered on students who "inquire, include, collaborate, curate, explore, and engage" (American Association of School Librarians 2017).

Common Core Language Arts Literacy Standards

CCSS.ELA-Literacy.RL.1.1 • Ask and answer questions about key details in a text.
CCSS.ELA-Literacy.RL.1.3 • Use illustrations and details in a story to describe its characters, setting, or events.
CCSS.ELA-Literacy.RL.1.7 • Use illustrations and details in a text to describe its key ideas.

Social Studies Standards C3

D2.Civ.l.K-2. Describe the roles and responsibilities of people in authority.
D2.Civ.2.K-2. Describe how all people have roles in a community.

Learning Objectives

Students will

- Recognize those in authority in a school and how their roles help students.
- Know the roles of the custodian, librarian, principal, and teacher and how they help students.
- Brainstorm how students could possibly help in a school too.
- Research locating details by using illustrations.

Suggested Teaching Team

School library and social studies teachers.

Instructional Procedure

Lessons will be a collaborative lesson for most of the class time. Teachers are always checking for understanding. Students are more often than not involved in paired or team work so that all learners have a chance to gather ideas and be involved. Assessment is ongoing observation.

1. Teachers will have students brainstorm a posted class list of the adults in the school who have authority in the school and who help in some way in the school.
2. Students will hear a nonfiction book that generalizes or groups all of those adults who help in a school. After hearing the book, more school helper authority roles and their jobs may be added to the list. Students will connect to their prior knowledge in order to be able to consider the job role for each added school helper.
3. To set the stage for researching, teachers will first need to explain to students that the words *custodian* and *janitor* mean the same. Likewise, the words *librarian*, *teacher librarian*, or *media specialist* mean the same person.
4. Student pairs or small groups will question (inquire), discuss (include), and gather information by browsing and exploring other nonfiction books for more evidence (curate) so as to better recognize

how those in authority in a school help. After five minutes, students will report their findings to the class and apply their learning.

5. When looking at the worksheets, class discussion will emphasize how those in authority help in a school: custodian (janitor), librarian, nurse, principal, and teacher. For instance, the principal runs the school and has lots of meetings to help with things.

6. When answering the worksheet, students will question and then match by connecting lines from the person in authority to how that school person helps. For instance, a custodian or janitor helps by keeping the school clean (vacuums). Students are applying their learning in an engaging way.

7. Students will need to draw themselves in the top box. For the bottom of the worksheet, teachers will tell students to brainstorm and then draw how they could help in a school too. While waiting for some students to finish, students will color their worksheets.

8. If time allows, teachers will read a fiction picture book on a teacher, principal, or librarian and discuss how the main character helped in the school.

Recommended Resources

Fiction

Bowen, Anne. *I Know an Old Teacher.* Minneapolis, MN: Carolrhoda, 2013.

Cocca-Leffler, Maryann. *Mr. Tanen's Ties Rule!* Morton Grove, IL: Albert Whitman & Company, 2003.

Dajos, Kalli, and Alicia Des Marteau. *Our Principal Promised to Kiss a Pig.* Morton Grove, IL: Albert Whitman & Company, 2014.

Finchler, Judy, and Kevin O'Malley. *Miss Malarkey Leaves No Reader Behind.* New York: Bloomsbury, 2010.

Hopkinson, Deborah. *A Letter to My Teacher.* New York: Schwartz & Wade, 2017.

Oilver, Llanit. *Olivia and the Best Teacher Ever.* New York: Simon & Schuster, 2012.

Tibbot, Julie. *Curious George, Librarian for a Day.* New York: Houghton Mifflin, 2012.

Nonfiction—General

Bullard, Lisa. *Who Works at Hannah's School?* Minneapolis, MN: Millbrook, 2017.

Coan, Susan. *Workers at My School.* Huntington Beach, CA: Teacher Created Materials, 2015.

Fronczak, Emerson. *Who Works at My School?* New York: Rosen, 2013.

Kidde, Rita. *Jobs in My School.* New York: PowerKids Press, 2015.

Preus, Janet. *People Who Help at School* [CD & Book]. North Mankato, MN: Cantata Learning, 2015.

Nonfiction—Custodians, Nurses, Librarians, Principals, and Teachers

Arnold, Quinn M. *Teachers.* Mankato, MN: Creative Education, 2018.

Bell, Samantha. *Teacher.* Ann Arbor, MI: Cherry Lake Publishing, 2019.

Bellisario, Gina, and Ed Myer. *Let's Meet a Librarian.* Minneapolis, MN: Millbrook, 2013.

Devera, Czeena. *Principal.* Ann Arbor, MI: Cherry Lake Publishing, 2018.

Gaertner, Meg. *Teachers.* Minneapolis, MN: Pop!, 2019.

Gaetano, Capici. *Principals.* Ann Arbor, MI: Cherry Lake Publishing, 2011.

Heos, Bridget. *Teachers in My Community.* Minneapolis, MN: Lerner, 2019.

Kidde, Rita. *What Do Teachers Do?* New York: PowerKids, 2014.

Kidde, Rita. *What Does a Janitor Do?* New York: PowerKids, 2014.

Kidde, Rita. *What Does the Principal Do?* New York: PowerKids, 2014.

Leaf, Christina. *Teachers.* Brunswick, MD: Bellwether Media, 2018.

Manley, Erika S. *Custodians.* Minneapolis, MN: Jump!, 2018.

Marsico, Katie. *Working at the Library.* Ann Arbor, MI: Cherry Lake Publishing, 2013.

McCune, Susan. *Mr. Morgan Keeps Our School Clean*. New York: Rosen, 2016.

McCune, Susan. *Our School Nurse*. New York: Rosen, 2016.

Miller, Heather. *Librarian*. Chicago, IL: Heinemann, 2002.

Moening, Kate. *Custodians*. Brunswick, MD: Bellwether Media, 2019.

Morris, Ann. *That's Our Librarian*. Minneapolis, MN: Millbrook Press, 2003.

Murray, Julie. *Librarians*. Mankato, MN: ABDO, 2010.

Murray, Julie. *Principals*. Mankato, MN: ABDO, 2019.

Murray, Julie. *Teachers*. Mankato, MN: ABDO, 2016.

Nelson, Robin. *Custodians*. Minneapolis, MN: Lerner, 2005.

Winston, Garrett. *What Does the School Nurse Do?* New York: PowerKids, 2015.

Rules and Laws

My Laws

My Rules

Laws

*Laws are made by government leaders.

*Laws are made to protect me and others.

Here is a law:

Rules

*Rules are made to make things fair for me and fair for others.

Here is a rule:

Start Here

STOP

Rules and Laws, Directions

Civics: Rules and laws
Grade Levels Suggested: Second Grade or First–Second Grades

Standards

AASL Standards

AASL Standards are listed at the start of each chapter, as each of those given standards are used in each lesson, as lessons are centered on students who "inquire, include, collaborate, curate, explore, and engage" (American Association of School Librarians 2017).

Common Core Language Arts Literacy Standards

CCSS.ELA-Literacy.RL.1.7 • Use illustrations and details in a story to describe its characters, setting, or events.
CCSS.ELA-Literacy.RI.2.1 • Ask and answer such questions as who, what, where, when, why, and how to demonstrate understanding of the key details in a text.

Social Studies Standards C3

D2.Civ.3.K-2. Describe the need for rules in and out of school.

Learning Objectives

Students will

- Recognize the differences between laws and rules in their community.
- Hear and discuss a fiction book on laws and rules, and discuss characters and plot.
- List a couple of laws and then some rules as applicable to them in their community.
- Question, explore, and locate laws and rules as it relates to them and their community.
- Each create and illustrate a laws and rules booklet.

Suggested Teaching Team

School library and social studies teachers.

Instructional Procedure

Lessons will be a collaborative lesson for most of the class time. Teachers are always checking for understanding. Students are more often than not involved in paired or team work so that all learners have a chance to gather ideas and be involved. Assessment is ongoing observation.

1. Teachers will write the words *laws* and *rules* at the top of a posted T-chart, with space to define those words first. Teachers will help students use prior knowledge to define a law versus a rule. For instance, rules solve problems and help everyone to be fair. Laws are made by government leaders and protect everyone.
2. Examples of laws are next. Teachers will guide students as they question (inquire) and use prior knowledge to state one to three laws that they may know from the T-chart, like stopping at a stop sign, wearing a helmet when riding a bike in many states, or wearing a seat belt in a car.
3. Then students will question, discuss rules (curate), reflect, and describe two rules seen in school, at home, and in their neighborhood. A few answers will be written on the class T-chart.

4. Student groups will quickly inquire, include, curate, collaborate, and explore nonfiction books on rules and laws in order to find one to two more rules or laws for the class T-chart. Engaged students will share their findings with the class.

5. Each student will apply their learning by creating a rules and laws booklet. Students will first illustrate or write a rule and a law. Students will illustrate their booklets, cut out their booklets, and attach the booklets together. The first stop sign is the cover, and the maze is the back cover.

6. If time permits, teachers will read a fiction picture book on rules or laws. Title, characters, and plot will be discussed by students, as well as the rule or law.

7. At the next class meeting, students will add a page on rules for using the internet or for being online at school. Note those suggested resources.

Recommended Resources

Fiction

Brannen, Sarah. S. *Madam Martine Breaks the Rules*. Park Ridge, IL: Albert Whitman & Company, 2015.

Cronin, Doreen. *Click, Clack, Quack to School!* New York: Atheneum Books, 2018.

Freidman, Laurie B., and Teresa Murfin. *Back-to-School Rules*. Minneapolis, MN: Carolrhoda Books, 2011.

LaFaye, Alexandria. *No Frogs in School*. New York: Sterling Children's Books, 2018.

Rey, Hans A. *Curious George Goes Swimming*. New York: Houghton Mifflin Harcourt, 2019.

Nonfiction

Alexander, Vincent. *Obeying Laws*. Minneapolis, MN: Pogo, 2019.

Booker, Dwayne. *Fiona Follows Schools Rules: Understanding Citizenship*. New York: Rosen, 2018.

Boothroyd, Jennifer. *What Are Rules and Laws?* Minneapolis, MN: Lerner Publications, 2015.

Collins, Savina. *Who Makes the Rules?* Vero Beach, FL: Rourke Educational Media, 2018.

Gorman, Jacqueline. *Why Do We Have Laws?* Milwaukee, WI: Gareth Stevens Publishers, 2008.

Javernick, Ellen, and Colleen M. Madden. *What If Everybody Did That?* New York: Two Lions, 2010.

Jeffries, Corina. *Citizenship at School: Understanding Citizenship*. New York: Rosen, 2018.

Kingsley, Thomas. *Staying Safe at School*. Mankato, MN: Capstone, 2019.

Kishel, Ann-Marie. *Rules and Laws*. Minneapolis, MN: Lerner Classroom, 2007.

Mayer, Cassie. *Following Rules*. Chicago, IL: Heinemann, 2018.

Nelson, Robin. *Following Rules*. Minneapolis, MN: Learner Classroom, 2003.

Pegis, Jessica. *Why Do We Need Rules and Laws?* New York: Crabtree, 2016.

Troupe, Thomas K. *Staying Safe at School*. Mankato, MN: Picture Window Books, 2019.

Nonfiction—Rules Online

ABCya.com. "Hippo and Hedgehog in Cyber-Five." Video. Updated 2019. http://www.abcya.com/cyber_five_internet_safety.htm.

Booker, Dwayne. *Rules for Using the Internet*. New York: Rosen, 2019.

Clasky, Leonard. *Ruby Follows Rules Following Rules Online*. New York: Rosen, 2019.

Common Sense Media. "5 Internet Safety Tips for Kids." Video. Updated 2016. https://www.youtube.com/watch?v=X9Htg8V3eik.

Harper, Reggie. *I Play by the Rules Following Rules Online*. New York: Rosen, 2018.

Huffman, Mindy. *My Teacher's Rules: Following Rules Online*. New York: Rosen, 2019.

Mayor

1. What is the main job of the mayor?

2. How could the mayor help with a problem in the city?

3. How does the mayor get the job as mayor?

4. Look at the city in the picture. What things could the mayor add to it to make it a better city?

   (1) Help the mayor. Draw things in the city to make it better.

   (2) Color the city to make it look beautiful.

Mayor, Directions

Civics: Government—mayor
Grade Levels Suggested: Second Grade or Second–First and Third Grades

Standards

AASL Standards

AASL Standards are listed at the start of each chapter, as each of those given standards are used in each lesson, as lessons are centered on students who "inquire, include, collaborate, curate, explore, and engage" (American Association of School Librarians 2017).

Common Core Language Arts Literacy Standards

CCSS.ELA-Literacy.RL.2.7 • Use information gained from the illustrations and words in a print or digital text to demonstrate understanding of its characters, setting, or plot.
CCSS.ELA-Literacy.RI.2.1 • Ask and answer such questions as who, what, where, when, why, and how to demonstrate understanding of the key details in a text.

Social Studies Standards C3

D2.Civ.l.K-2. Describe the roles and responsibilities of people in authority.
D.2.Civ.10.K-2. Compare own point of view with others

Learning Objectives

Students will

- Hear and discuss an easy fiction book about a mayor.
- Know what a city mayor does.
- Know how a city mayor is elected.
- Research a mayor's duties, and answer worksheet questions with the help of others.
- Help to create a better town for the mayor.

Suggested Teaching Team

School library and social studies teachers.

Instructional Procedure

Lessons will be a collaborative lesson for most of the class time. Teachers are always checking for understanding. Students are more often than not involved in paired or team work so that all learners have a chance to gather ideas and be involved. Assessment is ongoing observation.

1. Teachers will briefly discuss student ideas from prior knowledge about what the mayor does and write the ideas on a classroom board display.
2. Teachers will read a fiction picture book on a mayor and discuss the character with the help of students. The role of a mayor seen in the fiction book will be discussed as possible roles for a mayor.
3. Small student groups will then question (inquire), include all group learners, and collaborate, curate, and gather information from a nonfiction book in order to solve the first three worksheet problems with engaged learning.
4. Question three may need teacher guidance. With assistance, students will recognize how the mayor is elected in a city election.

5. Individual students will design a better city on the worksheet for the mayor. For instance, they would draw a fire station, a police station, a stop sign, and flowers in one of the flower containers to make the city look better and perhaps add a tree, roads, and more. They could create a welcome to the city sign and give the city a name.

6. Teachers will lead a class discussion on the worksheet answers to better apply new learning, including how students helped to make the city a better place. Students may express their own points of view.

7. A follow-up class would be conducted to briefly discuss the city council's roles. Resources are given, if needed.

Recommended Resources

Fiction

Berenstain, Jan. *The Berenstain Bears and Mama for Mayor*. New York: Harper, 2012.

Grambling, Lois G. *Can I Bring Saber to New York City, Ms. Mayor?* Watertown, MA: Charlesbridge, 2014.

Martinez, Manuel. *I Meet the Mayor*. New York: Rosen, 2019.

Nakamura, May. *The Cat Who Ruled the Town*. New York: Simon Spotlight, 2019.

Smith, James A. *The Monster Mayor*. Austin, TX: Number 6 Press, 2017.

Tomorrow, Tom. *The Very Silly Mayor*. New York: Ig Publishing, 2009.

Nonfiction

Armentrout, David. *The Major's Office*. Chicago, IL: Britannica, 2013.

Brody, Morgan. *City Council Member*. Newark, DE: Mitchell Lane Publishers, 2018.

Brody, Morgan. *Mayor*. Newark, DE: Mitchell Lane Publishers, 2018.

DeGezelle, Terri. *The City Council*. Minneapolis, MN: Capstone, 2015.

Gorman, Jacqueline L. *Mayor*. Milwaukee, WI: Gareth Stevens, 2009.

Harris, Nancy. *What's a City Council*. Chicago, IL: Heinemann, 2007.

Harris, Nancy. *What's a Mayor?* Chicago, IL: Heinemann, 2007.

Jakubiak, David J. *What Does a Mayor Do?* New York: PowerKids Press, 2010.

Jeffries, Joyce. *Meet the Mayor/Conoce A Los Alcaldes* [Bilingual]. New York: Gareth Stevens, 2013.

Manley, Erika. *Mayors*. Minneapolis, MN: Jump!, 2017.

Manning, Jack. *The City Mayor*. Minneapolis, MN: Capstone, 2015.

Morgan, Brody. *Mayor*. Newark, DE: Mitchell Lane Publishers, 2018.

Murray, Julie. *Mayor*. Mankato, MN: ABDO, 2018.

Silvia, Sadie. *What Does the Mayor Do? Understanding Government*. New York: Rosen, 2019.

What Does a Governor Do?

As governor, I would:

1. Who is your state governor? _____

2. The state governor is the head of your state. List or draw three governor jobs.

3. There are three branches of the state government. Those three branches are the:

(1) _____ branch to make laws, the

(2) _____ branch for the state court system, and the

(3) _____ branch for the governor and some others.

4. Become the governor. In the preceding box, list or draw things that you would do as the state governor.

What Does a Governor Do? Directions

Civics: State government
Grade Levels Suggested: Third Grade or Third–Fifth Grades

Standards

AASL Standards

AASL Standards are listed at the start of each chapter, as each of those given standards are used in each lesson, as lessons are centered on students who "inquire, include, collaborate, curate, explore, and engage" (American Association of School Librarians 2017).

Common Core Language Arts Literacy Standards

CCSS.ElA-Literacy.RI.3.1 • Ask and answer questions to demonstrate understanding of a text, referring explicitly to the text for answers.

Social Studies Standards C3

D2.Civ.1.3-5. Know responsibilities and powers of government officials.
D2.Civ.10.3-5. Identify beliefs, experiences, outlook, and values of own and others views on civic issues.

Learning Objectives

Students will

- Discuss and recognize the powers and responsibilities of a state governor.
- Become aware of the three branches of the state government by research.
- Consider what things they would do as state governor.
- Research governor roles using nonfiction sources.

Suggested Teaching Team

School library and social studies teachers.

Instructional Procedure

Lessons will be a collaborative student lesson for most of the class time. Students are more often than not involved in paired or team work so that all learners have a chance to gather ideas and be involved. Assessment is ongoing observation while also checking for understanding.

1. Teachers will introduce the lesson by first asking who is the state governor. Students will research quickly to name their state governor on the classroom display board.
2. Teachers will introduce the three branches of the state government by writing the following terms on the classroom display board: *executive*, *judicial*, and *legislative branches*. Using nonfiction resources, student groups will be given three to four minutes to question, collaborate with others, gather information, explore, and engage to see how the three branches work together and what they do. Students will share that information with the class.
3. Then, student groups will question, curate, and explore the state governor jobs. Those results will be shared with the class.
4. Student pairs will answer the worksheet. They will also draw or write what things they would do as a student governor. Some will share this information with the class.

5. If time permits, teachers will briefly share online information about how students actually can become a governor for a day (see the Connecticut links).

Recommended Resources

Nonfiction

Alexander, Vincent. *State Government*. Minneapolis, MN: Pogo, 2019.

Connecticut's Kid Governor. "Kid Governor." Updated 2017. http://www.kidgovernor.org/.

Connecticut Public Affairs Network. "Oregon's Kid Governor." Updated 2019. http://orkg. kidgovernor.org.

George, Patrick E. "How State Governors Work." Updated 2018. https://people.howstuffworks. com/government/local-politics/state-governor1.htm.

Giesecke, Ernestine. *State Government* (Kids' Guide to Government). Chicago, IL: Heinemann, 2009.

Jakubiak, David. J. *What Does a Governor Do?* New York: PowerKids Press, 2010.

Machajewski, Sarah. *What Are State and Local Governments?* Chicago, IL: Britannica Educational, 2015.

Mahoney, Emily J. *Becoming a State Governor*. Milwaukee, WI: Gareth Stevens, 2016.

Murray, Julie. *Governor*. Mankato, MN: Abdo Kids, 2018.

I Have Voted!

1. Suppose you were an American citizen, and you voted in an election. How old would you be? _____

2. Why is it important to vote for a government leader or vote on other things?

_____

_____

_____

_____

3. Describe the book you read on voting.

Title: _____

Author: _____

Describe what you learned about voting from the book: _____

_____

_____

_____

_____

4. If you agree that it is important to vote, cut out the voting badge and wear it!

I Have Voted! Directions

Civics: Voting
Grade Levels Suggested: Third Grade or Third–Fifth Grades

Standards

AASL Standards

AASL Standards are listed at the start of each chapter, as each of those given standards are used in each lesson, as they are centered on students who "inquire, include, collaborate, curate, explore, and engage" (American Association of School Librarians 2017).

Common Core Language Arts Literacy Standards

CCSS.ELA-Literacy.RL.3.1 • Ask and answer questions to demonstrate understanding of a text, referring explicitly to the text as the basis for the answers.

CCSS.ELA-Literacy.RL.3.3 • Describe characters in a story (e.g., their traits, motivations, or feelings), and explain how their actions contribute to the sequence of events.

CCSS.ELA-Literacy.RI.3.7 • Use information gained from illustrations (e.g., maps and photographs) and the words in a text to demonstrate understanding of the text (e.g., where, when, why, and how key events occur).

Social Studies Standards C3

D2.Civ.2.3-5. Describe how a democracy relies on people to participate.

D2.Civ.10.3-5. Identify beliefs, experiences, outlook, and values of own and others' views on civic issues.

Learning Objectives

Students will

- Become aware of the value of voting and basic voting requirements.
- Research nonfiction voting books.
- Examine illustrations for facts.
- Skim a quick reading fiction or nonfiction picture-type book about voting, and share that information on a worksheet and with others. Title, author, and main character will be discussed.

Suggested Teaching Team

School library and social studies teachers.

Instructional Procedure

Lessons will be a collaborative lesson for most of the class time. Students are more often than not involved in paired or team work so that all learners have a chance to gather ideas and be involved. Assessment is ongoing observation while also checking for understanding.

1. Teachers will very briefly introduce the voting lesson by asking for a vote on anything related to school so that students can connect voting to prior knowledge, like including something on the school lunch menu. Then teachers will ask students to explain the purpose of voting and why it is important.

2. On the class board or classroom display board, teachers will define what enables one to vote and why adults vote.

3. For four to five minutes, student pairs will question or inquire, explore while including all views, collaborate, and then skim (curate and explore) nonfiction books to gather information on voting in the United States, including the importance of voting. Engaged students will share some of that information, which will be briefly written on the classroom display board.

4. Student pairs will skim a voting picture book–type format that is fiction or nonfiction. Students will reflect and answer their worksheet questions. Worksheet answers will show the author, title and main plot and briefly discuss outlooks on voting.

5. If time permits, student pairs will share their stories and worksheet answers with another pair or with a small group.

6. Students will color the voting badge, cut it out, and wear it.

Recommended Resources

Nonfiction

Anderson, Nancy. *Citizens Vote in a Democracy.* New York: Rosen, 2017.

Bonwill, Ann. *We Can Vote.* Chicago, IL: Children's Press, 2019.

Carson, Mary K. *Why Couldn't Susan B. Anthony Vote? And Other Questions about Women's Suffrage.* New York: Sterling Children's Books, 2015.

Christelow, Eileen. *Vote!* New York: Houghton Mifflin Harcourt, 2018.

De Capua, Sarah. *Voting!* New York: Scholastic, 2013.

Gillibrand, Kristen. *Bold & Brave: Ten Heroes Who Won Women the Right to Vote.* New York: Alfred A. Knopf, 2018.

Hunt, Santana. *Why Do We Vote?* Milwaukee, WI: Gareth Stevens, 2018.

Landau, Elaine. *Women's Rights to Vote.* Chicago, IL: Children's Press, 2007.

Nelson, Kristen R. *What Is Voting?* New York: PowerKids Press, 2019.

Nelson, Kristen R. *Why Should People Vote?* New York: PowerKids Press, 2018.

Shamir, Ruby. *What's the Big Deal about Election?* New York: Philomel Books, 2018.

Picture Book Format—Fiction and Nonfiction

Anastasia, Suen. *Vote for Isaiah! A Citizenship Story.* Minneapolis, MN: Magic Wagon, 2009.

Bandy, Michael S. *Granddaddy's Turn: A Journey to the Ballot Box.* Somerville, MA: Candlewick, 2015.

Lee, Tanya. *Elizabeth Leads the Way: Elizabeth Cady Stanton and the Right to Vote.* New York: Henry Holt, 2008.

Murphy, Claire R. *Marching with Aunt Susan.* Atlanta, GA: Peachtree, 2017.

Rapport, Doreen. *Elizabeth Started All the Trouble.* New York: Hyperion, 2016.

Robbins, Dean. *Miss Paul and the President: The Creative Campaign for Women's Right to Vote.* New York: Alfred A. Knopf, 2016.

Rockliff, Mara. *Around America to Win the Vote: Two Suffragists, Kitten, and 10,000 Miles.* Somerville, MA: Candlewick, 2016.

Stone, Tanya L. *Elizabeth Leads the Way: Elizabeth Leads the Way.* New York: Henry Holt and Company, 2010.

Winter, Jonah. *Lillian's Right to Vote.* New York: Schwartz & Wade Books, 2015.

Bill of Rights

1. Why were the Bill of Rights added to the U.S. Constitution?

2. Create a First Amendment poster.

(A) Gather ideas. In your own words, list and briefly describe the four rights of the First Amendment.

(B) Then colorfully write the four rights on a First Amendment poster. Decorate it.

Bill of Rights, Directions

Civics: Bill of rights
Grade Levels Suggested: Fourth Grade or Third–Fifth Grades

Standards

AASL Standards

AASL Standards are listed at the start of each chapter, as each of those given standards are used in each lesson, as lessons are centered on students who "inquire, include, collaborate, curate, explore, and engage" (American Association of School Librarians 2017).

Common Core Language Arts Literacy Standards

CCSS.ELA-Literacy.R.I.5.9 • Integrate information from several texts on the same topic in order to write or speak about the subject knowledgeably.

Social Studies Standards C3

D2.Civ.1.3-5. Know responsibilities and powers of government officials.
D2.Civ.5.3-5. Look at the origin and purpose of rules, laws, and the U.S. Constitution.

Learning Objectives

Students will

- Recognize the rights given in the Bill of Rights.
- Create a poster on the First Amendment.
- Gather some ideas and information from multiple sources.
- View an online Bill of Rights video and discuss it.
- Student groups will research the Bill of Rights from nonfiction sources in order to be able to define those amendments in their own words.
- Answer their worksheets, including the creation of a mini poster.

Suggested Teaching Team

School library and social studies teachers.

Instructional Procedure

Lessons will be a collaborative lesson for most of the class time. Students are more often than not involved in paired or team work so that all learners have a chance to gather ideas and be so involved. Assessment is ongoing observation while also checking for understanding.

1. Teachers will first help students understand that the U.S. Constitution is the foundation for the American government. The Constitution has additions or amendments. The first ten amendments concern our rights, which is why they are called the Bill of Rights.
2. Teachers will show an online video on the Bill of Rights. Teachers will then lead a brief discussion to answer the first worksheet question from the video information.
3. Student groups will first briefly question (inquire), include and collaborate other views, and curate (gather information) and research with a nonfiction book or an online source on what is in the First Amendment.

4. On worksheets student groups will briefly summarize the First Amendment rights by listing and briefly describing them in their own words. Students will share results with the class. Teachers will also ask students how the First Amendment could be applied to them.

5. Individuals or paired students will create a mini First Amendment worksheet poster. Students will colorfully state the four First Amendment rights on the poster. If desired, students could use the pictures at the top of their worksheets for their poster or create their own pictures.

6. If some students have time, they could play an online constitution game or simply help others.

7. As a follow-up lesson, teachers will read to the class a picture book on either the freedom of speech or the freedom of assembly and discuss how those books will apply to people.

Recommended Resources

Fiction

Freedom of Speech

Deedy, Carmen A. *The Rooster Who Would Not Be Quiet*. New York: Scholastic, 2017.

Freedom of Assembly

Farris, Christine K. *March On! The Day My Brother Martin Changed the World*. New York: Scholastic, 2008.

Markel, Michelle. *Brave Girl: Clara and the Shirtwaist Makers' Strike of 1909*. New York: Balzer & Bray, 2013.

Weatherford, Carole B. *Voice of Freedom: Fannie Lou Hamer: The Spirit of the Civil Rights Movement*. Somerville, MA: The Candlewick, 2015.

Nonfiction

Dils, Tracey E. *12 Questions about the Bill of Rights (Examining Primary Sources)*. Mankato, MN: 12-Story Library, 2016.

Freedom Factor. "The Constitution for Kids—Bill of Rights." Video. Updated 2018. https://www.youtube.com/watch?v=3P6E3Bpn5yw

Homeschool Pop. "The Bill of Rights for Kids." Video. Updated 2018. https://www.youtube.com/watch?v=7dSyMG8OJcYchool.

Interactive Constitution [Game]. https://constitutioncenter.org/interactive-constitution?gclid=EAIaIQobChMIu6ujya2y3wIVCkNpCh2LAwsOEAMYAiAAEgJu-vD_BwE#.

Isaacs, Sally S. *Understanding the Bill of Rights*. New York: Crabtree, 2009.

Krull, Kathleen, and Anna DiVito. *A Kids' Guide to America's Bill of Rights*. Revised edition. New York: HarperCollins, 2015.

Lynch, Seth. *The Bill of Rights*. Milwaukee, WI: Gareth Stevens Publishing, 2018.

Machajewski, Sarah. *American Freedom's: A Look at the First Amendment*. New York: PowerKids Press, 2019.

Metz, Lorijo. *The United States Constitution and the Bill of Rights*. New York: PowerKids Press, 2014.

Micklos, John. *The First Amendment: Freedom of Speech and Religion*. North Mankato, MN: Capstone Press, 2017.

Micklos, John Jr., and Kristin W. Larson. *Cause and Effect: The Bill of Rights: Freedom Of Speech and Religions*. Minneapolis, MN: Capstone Press, 2017.

Rokutani, John. *Freedom of Speech, the Press, and Religion: The First Amendment (The Bill of Rights)*. Berkeley Heights, NJ: Enslow, 2017.

Smart Songs. "Bill of Rights Rap—Smart Songs." Video. Updated 2009. https://www.youtube.com/watch?v=tlt6R1KD4E0.

We the People

Write an amendment.

1. Briefly describe the purpose of the U.S. Constitution.

2. List the three main parts of the U.S. Constitution.

3. List the three government branches stated in the U.S. Constitution.

4. On the following document, add an amendment to the Constitution for others.

We the People of the United States,

We the People, Directions

Civics: Learning about the U.S. Constitution basics
Grade Levels Suggested: Fourth Grade or Third–Fifth Grades

Standards

AASL Standards

AASL Standards are listed at the start of each chapter, as each of those given standards are used in each lesson, as they are centered on students who "inquire, include, collaborate, curate, explore, and engage" (American Association of School Librarians 2017).

Common Core Language Arts Literacy Standards

CCSS.ElA-Literacy.RI.4.1 • Refer to details and examples in a text, when explaining what the text says explicitly and when drawing inferences from the text.
CCSS.ELA-Literacy.RI.4.7 • Interpret information presented visually, orally, or quantitatively (e.g., in charts, graphs, diagrams, timelines, animations, or interactive elements on web pages), and explain how the information contributes to an understanding of the text in which it appears.

Social Studies Standards C3

D2.Civ.5.3-5. Look at the origin and purpose of rules, laws, and the U.S. Constitution.
D2.Civ.10.3-5. Identify beliefs, experiences, outlook, and values of own and others views on civic issues.

Learning Objectives

Students will

- Be able to describe a basic understanding of the U.S. Constitution purpose, the three main parts, and the three government branches.
- Research in groups to find facts on the Constitution using online videos.
- Research in groups to create Constitution questions, and then answer those questions using nonfiction books.
- Work with another to write their own amendment on the worksheet document and answer worksheet questions.

Suggested Teaching Team

School library and social studies teachers.

Instructional Procedure

Lessons will be a collaborative lesson for most of the class time. Teachers are always checking for understanding. Students are more often than not involved in paired or team work so that all learners have a chance to gather ideas and be involved. Assessment is ongoing observation.

1. Teachers will briefly describe the purpose of the U.S Constitution.
2. Student groups will select a group recorder to record groups' facts. Student groups will question (inquire), connect to prior knowledge, draw on inferences, discuss and include others and collaborate in the group, research (curate), and include their views, as they are answering the first three worksheet questions from an online video or nonfiction book. Students will write something like the following. There are three Constitution parts: preamble (the introduction), the articles (basic

government rules), and then the amendments (constitution changes). They will also briefly list the three government branches.

3. Students and teachers will briefly discuss some of the very basic rights seen in the amendments and the impact on them.

4. Teachers will need to guide student work for the last worksheet question. Student pairs will collaborate and very neatly write their own amendment that would benefit others. Student pairs will share their work with other student pairs.

5. If time allows, student pairs will consider what else they learned and then want to know regarding the Constitution and finally research a nonfiction book to locate the answers. Student pairs will share their answers with other student pairs.

Recommended Resources

Nonfiction

Burgan, Michael. *Cornerstones of Freedom: The U.S. Constitution*. New York: Scholastic, 2011.

Catrow, David. *We the Kids: The Preamble to the Constitution of the United States*. Estes Park, CO: Puffin, 2005.

Clay, Kathryn. *The U.S. Constitution: Introducing Primary Sources*. North Mankato, MN: Capstone, 2017.

Freedom Factor. "The Constitution for Kids—Who Makes the Rules?" Video. Updated 2018. https://www.youtube.com/watch?v=NmwzK1Ba7v0.

Higgins, Nadia. *US Government through Infographics*. Minneapolis, MN: Lerner, 2013.

Homeschool Pop. "Constitution Facts for Kids." Video. Updated 2018. https://www.youtube.com/watch?v=6gVAhjl5_6E.

Lusted, Marica A. *The U.S. Constitution*. Mankato, MN: Child's World, 2016.

Mount, Bruce. "U.S. Constitution." Video. Updated 2012. https://www.usconstitution.net/constkids4.html.

Shmoop. "The Constitution." Video. Updated 2015. https://www.youtube.com/watch?v=9mP-nkFg5_E.

Steinkraus. Kyla. *Constitution*. Vero Beach, FL: Rourke Educational Media, 2014.

Time for Kids, eds. *Our Nation's Documents: The Written Words That Shaped Our Country*. New York: Time Inc. Books, 2018.

United States Printing Office. "U.S. Constitution: 1789." https://bensguide.gpo.gov/u-s-constitution-1789.

Declaration of Independence

1. What does the Fourth of July have to do with the Declaration of Independence?

2. Why was the Declaration of Independence written?

3. In your opinion, what do the following Declaration of Independence words mean today: "All men are created equal"?

4. What do these Declaration of Independence words mean today: "All have certain rights like life, liberty, and the pursuit (search) for happiness"?

5. Create a three- to four-line Declaration of Independence poem below.

Declaration of Independence, Directions

Civics: Impact of Declaration of Independence
Grade Levels Suggested: Fifth Grade or Fifth Grade or Older

Standards

AASL Standards

AASL Standards are listed at the start of each chapter, as each of those given standards are used in each lesson, as lessons are centered on students who "inquire, include, collaborate, curate, explore, and engage" (American Association of School Librarians 2017).

Common Core Language Arts Literacy Standards

CCSS.ELA-Literacy.RI.5.7 • Draw on information from multiple print or digital sources, demonstrating the ability to locate an answer to a question quickly or to solve a problem efficiently.
CCSS.ELA-Literacy.R.I.5.9 • Integrate information from several texts on the same topic in order to write or speak about the subject knowledgeably.

Social Studies Standards C3

D2.Civ.10.3-5. Identify beliefs, experiences, outlook, and values of own and others views on civic issues.

Learning Objectives

Students will

- Recognize the background of the Declaration of Independence.
- Know the probable date of the Declaration and relate that date to today.
- Understand the truths of life, liberty, and pursuit of happiness equally for all, today.
- Use multiple sources in small groups to view and then discuss their findings from an online video and then from print books.
- Work in student pairs to answer their worksheet questions and write a poem.

Suggested Teaching Team

School library and social studies teachers.

Instructional Procedure

Lessons will be a collaborative lesson for most of the class time. Teachers are always checking for understanding. Students are more often than not involved in paired or team work so that all learners have a chance to gather ideas and be involved. Assessment is ongoing observation.

This lesson may require two sessions with students.

1. Students will view a Declaration of Independence online video.
2. Teachers will lead the class in discussing when the Declaration of Independence was accepted and ask if there was a reason why it was written. Those answers will be displayed on the class board.
3. For about five minutes, student small groups will question or inquire, connect to prior knowledge, include the group and collaborate, curate or explore sources, and then reflect on the Declaration of Independence meanings of the words about all men being created equal and life, liberty, and pursuit of happiness rights for all.

4. Teachers will lead a brief class discussion on the group results.

5. Student pairs will create a three- to four-line poem. If desired, students could use these poem words at the start of each line and then finish those thoughts: (1) all men are created equal, (2) all have life and liberty rights, and (3) all have the right to pursue happiness. They will create a poem title but can cut out and use the page title in the poem box also.

Recommended Resources

Nonfiction

Castellanao, Peter. *The Declaration of Independence*. Milwaukee, IL: Gareth Stevens, 2018.

Clay, Kathryn. *The Declaration of Independence*. Minneapolis, MN: Capstone, 2018.

Educational Network. "Biography: Thomas Jefferson for Kids (Cartoons). Declaration of Independence." Video. Updated 2015. https://www.youtube.com/watch?v=IPeffaxcT4k.

Harris, Michael C. *What Is the Declaration of Independence?* New York: Grosset & Dunlap, 2016.

Isaacs, Sally S. *Understanding the Declaration of Independence*. New York: Crabtree, 2008.

Leavitt, Amie J. *The Declaration of Independence in Translation: What It Really Means to Me*. Minneapolis, MN: Capstone 2017.

Levine, Becky. *For Life and Liberty: Causes and Effects of the Declaration of the Independence*. Minneapolis, MN: Capstone Press, 2014.

Liberty's Kids 114. "The First Fourth of July." Video. Updated 2016. https://www.youtube.com/watch?v=LK3Cs8EgOQo.

McDaniel, Melissa. *The Declaration of Independence (Cornerstones of Freedom)*. Chicago, IL: Children's Press, 2011.

Miller, Mirella S. *12 Questions about the Declaration of Independence (Examining Primary Sources)*. Mankato, MN: 12-Story Library, 2017.

Niver, Heather M. *20 Fun Facts about the Declaration of Independence*. Milwaukee, WI: Gareth Stevens, 2014.

School House Rock. "Schoolhouse Rock: Fireworks (Declaration of Independence)." Video. Updated 2015. https://www.youtube.com/watch?v=ZCkfa3pqihU.

Shea, John. *The Declaration of Independence*. Milwaukee, WI: Gareth Stevens, 2014.

Surfnetkids. "Effects of the Declaration of Independence Today." Updated 2018. https://www.surfnetkids.com/independenceday/268/effects-of-the-declaration-of-independence/.

Time for Kids, eds. *Our Nation's Documents*. Tampa, FL: Time for Kids, 2018.

Three Branches

The Three Branches Game

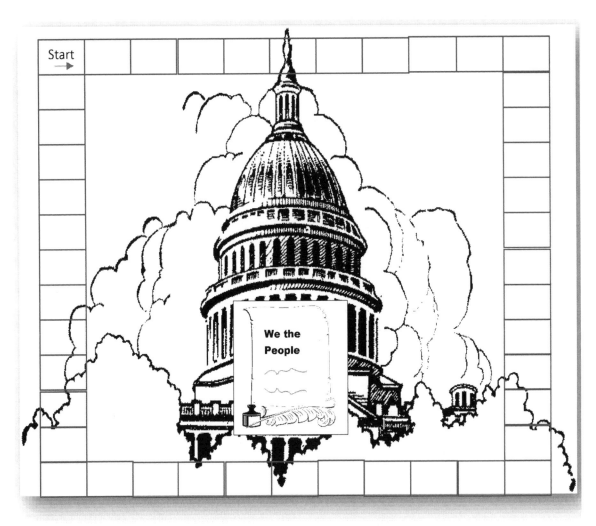

What are the three government branches?	What are the two parts of the legislative branch?	Who heads the executive branch?	Which branch writes laws?	Which branch has the Supreme Court?	Which branch has the Congress?	How could the Supreme Court balance government powers?
What document created the three branches?	How could a president balance a branch?	In early America, why was a constitution made?	Why are government powers shared?			

Three Branches, Directions

Civics: Three branches of the federal government and the U.S. Constitution
Grade Levels Suggested: Fifth Grade or Fourth–Fifth Grades

Standards

AASL Standards

AASL Standards are listed at the start of each chapter, as each of those given standards are used in each lesson, as they are centered on students who "inquire, include, collaborate, curate, explore, and engage" (American Association of School Librarians 2017).

Common Core Language Arts Literacy Standards

CCSS.ELA-Literacy.RI.5.7 • Draw on information from multiple print or digital sources, demonstrating the ability to locate an answer to a question quickly or to solve a problem efficiently.
CCSS.ELA-Literacy.R.I.5.9 • Integrate information from several texts on the same topic in order to write or speak about the subject knowledgeably.

Social Studies Standards C3

D2.Civ.1.3-5. Know responsibilities and powers of government officials.
D2.Civ.5.3-5. Look at the origin and purpose of rules, laws, and the U.S. Constitution.

Learning Objectives

Students will

- Hear a brief background discussing why the Constitution was written.
- Work in groups to explore and question the roles of the three federal government branches.
- Discover how the three federal government branches balance each other.
- Work in pairs to play the three branches and constitution game.
- Use multiple information sources.

Suggested Teaching Team

School library and social studies teachers.

Instructional Procedure

Lessons will be a collaborative lesson for most of the class time. Teachers are always checking for understanding. Students are more often than not involved in paired or team work so that all learners have a chance to gather ideas and be involved. Assessment is ongoing observation.

1. Students will eventually play a game. The worksheet game questions are seen under the game on the worksheet. First, teachers have the option to create more question cards in the empty spaces. Coins will be needed. The game sheet would also work better if printed on card stock.
2. Teachers will give a very brief basic background of why the Constitution was written and how that is reflected in the government powers.
3. For a few minutes, student groups will inquire, include all in the group, and then explore nonfiction or online sources in order to find basic facts that answer the game questions. The groups will briefly share their results with the class. This will prepare them for the game.
4. Student pairs will play another pair in the game.

5. The game board with the eagle and flag game markers will be cut out. The question cards below the game including any additional teacher question cards will be cut out and placed facedown. A coin flip will show the players how to process on the game board. If the coin flip shows heads, students will go ahead one, if answering correctly. If the coin toss shows tails, students will move two spaces, only if answering the question correctly.

6. Student pairs will finally become actively engaged by playing the three branches game with another pair. If no team has won after answering all game questions, the questions will be mixed up and answered again until someone wins. Teachers will monitor game answers, until someone in a student pair has reached the end or where they started.

Possible answers for the game are as follows:

Three government branches that balance power: executive, judicial, and legislative.

Two main parts of the Congress or legislative branch: Senate and House.

President heads the executive branch.

Legislative branch writes laws.

U.S. Supreme Court is in the judicial branch.

The branch that has the Congress is legislative.

Supreme Court balances power by being able to say a law may not be constitutional.

The Constitution created the three branches and defines what each branch is supposed to do.

The president balances the three-branch powers by appointing Supreme Court judges and can veto (not agree with) a law.

A constitution was made in early American times to set up the first government and give people rights and the power to balance the power.

Recommended Resources

Nonfiction

Brennan, Patricia. *What Is the Constitution?* New York: Penguin, 2013.

Buchanan, Shelly. *Our Government: The Three Branches.* Huntington Beach, CA: Teacher Created Materials, 2014.

Burgan, Michael. *The Branches of the U.S. Government.* New York: Scholastic, 2011.

"Liberty's Kids #40 We the People." Video. [Video showing colonist, early America and the constitution.]. Updated 2013. https://www.youtube.com/watch?v=Ceb1wkSamG4.

Lusted, Marcia A. *The U.S. Constitution (How America Works).* North Mankato, MN: Child's World, 2017.

Maestro, Betsy. *A More Perfect Union: The Story of Our Constitution.* New York: HarperCollins, 2008.

Morley, Jacqueline. *You Wouldn't Want to Be an American Colonist!* Chicago, IL: Children's Press, 2013.

Rajczak, Kristen. *Life in the American Colonies.* Milwaukee, WI: Gareth Stevens, 2013.

Richmond, Benjamin. *What Are the Three Branches of the Government: And Other Questions about . . . the U.S. Constitution.* New York: Sterling Children's Books, 2014.

Senzell, Sally. *All about America: Colonists and Independence.* London: Kingfisher, 2011.

Swain, Gwenyth. *Documents of Freedom: A Look at the Declaration of Impendence, the Bill of Rights, and the U.S. Constitution.* Minneapolis, MN: Lerner, 2012.

Taylor-Butler, Christine. *The Constitution.* Chicago, IL: Children's Press, 2008.

Thomas, William. *What Are the Parts of Government?* Milwaukee, WI: Gareth Stevens, 2008.

USA Gov. "Branches of the U.S. Government." https://www.usa.gov/branches-of-government.

Chapter 2

School Library and Social Studies Teachers with Economics

This chapter covers topics of economics taken from Social Studies Standards, along with library literacy standards and language arts standards. The elementary school librarians or teacher librarians partner with the elementary social studies teachers to provide excellence in education with engaging lessons, with library resources and online resources, as students collaborate with others in order to create learning. Lessons are approximately twenty minutes long and packed with resources, all based on standards.

If not using those standards, the educator can apply others. Likewise, the educator can pick and choose any of the three sets of standards—the library standards, Social Studies Standards, and language arts standards—or use all of those standards as applied to each lesson.

This chapter begins with lessons for kindergarten, with those lessons being usable for other lower elementary grades, and then the lessons move upward to the fifth grade. Grade levels are not narrowly assigned per lesson but are suggested. Furthermore, this book not only engages all learners but also offers lessons that can be intermingled for other elementary grades. There are many resources that have been tested before being suggested with each lesson, offering more teaching opportunities.

Standards

AASL Standards Framework

AASL Standards for Learners are listed at the start of each chapter, as each of those given standards are used in each lesson, as they are centered on students who "inquire, include, collaborate, curate, explore, and engage."

American Association of School Librarians. "AASL Standards Framework for Learners." Updated 2017. https://standards.aasl.org/framework.

AASL Standards Framework for Learners encourage learners to

1. Inquire through such means as questioning, using evidence, connecting to prior knowledge, making decisions, and more.
2. Include through such means as discussing, examining other's views, reflecting, and more.
3. Collaborate through participating, obtaining feedback, solving problems with others to connect shared learning, and more.
4. Curate through such means as determining a need and then gathering and organizing information from a variety of accurate resources, reflecting, and more.
5. Explore through such means as reading, writing, creating, asking questions, solving problems, expressing being curious, reflecting, and more.
6. Engage through such means as applying and evaluating information and sources to learning in an ethical way, including avoiding plagiarism and more.

Excerpted and adapted from *National School Library Standards for Learners, School Librarians, and School Libraries* by the American Association of School Librarians, a division of the American Library Association, copyright © 2018 American Library Association. Available for download at https://standards.aasl.org/framework. Used with permission.

Social Studies Standards—the Inquiry Arc of the C3 (College, Career, and Civic Life) Framework

Economics K-2

D2.Eco.1.K-2. Explain how scarcity makes decisions (This standard is for fourth grade as well as for K-2).

D2.Eco.2.K-2. Know the benefits and cost of personal decisions.

D2.Eco.4.K-2. Describe goods and services of local community people.

D2.Eco.6.K-2. Explain how people earn money.

D2.Eco.9.K-2. Explain the role of banks.

D2.Eco.10.K-2. Explain saving.

Economics 3-5

D2.Eco.1.3-5. Know the positive and negative costs of choices.

D2.Eco.3.3-5. Identify variety of resources like human capital, physical capital, and natural resources to make goods and services.

D2.Eco.10.3-5. Explain interest rates.

D2.Eco.12.3-5. Explain the ways that government pays for the goods and services it gives.

D2.Eco.14.K-2. Describe why people trade goods and services with other countries.

National Council for the Social Studies. *Social Studies for the Next Generation: Purposes, Practices, and Implications of the College, Career, and Civic Life (C3) Framework for Social Studies State Standards.* Silver Spring, MD. 2013.

Common Core Standards—Literacy

Common Course Language Arts Literacy Standards or CCSS, which are given in the introductory standards section of the book, are seen with each lesson. These standards are too lengthy to be given here at the start of each chapter, but they are seen as needed for each lesson. For a complete look at this book's Common Core Standards in Literacy, refer to the introduction section.

Educators may prefer to use other or additional standards or simply select some or all of the given standards. Each lesson holds a wealth of resources for educators to pick and choose from to support the standards-based learning lessons. The standards are the foundation or framework of learning, but the teachers hold the key.

Need or Want?

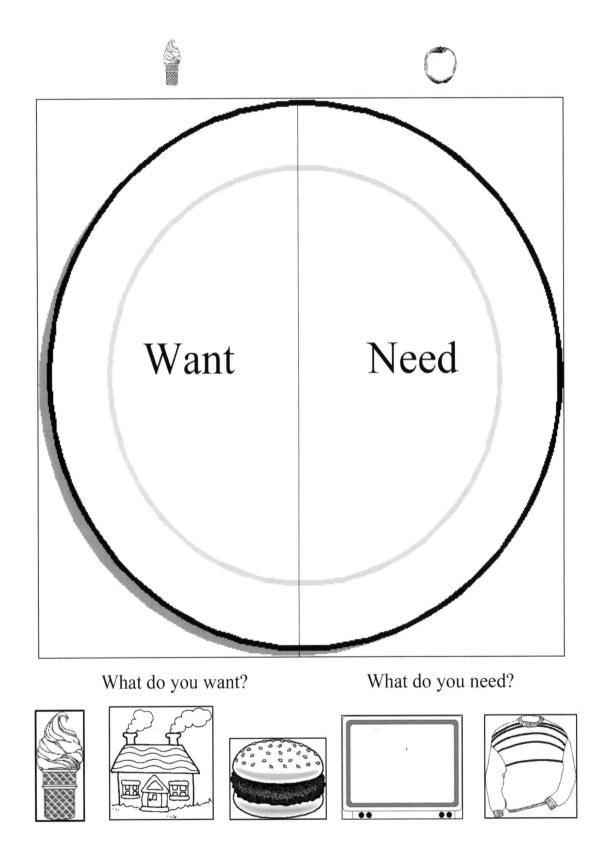

Want   Need

What do you want?   What do you need?

Need or Want? Directions

Economics: Need or want?
Grade Levels Suggested: Kindergarten or Kindergarten–Second Grades

Standards

AASL Standards

AASL Standards are listed at the start of each chapter, as each of those given standards are used in each lesson, as lessons are centered on students who "inquire, include, collaborate, curate, explore, and engage" (American Association of School Librarians 2017).

Common Core Language Arts Literacy Standards

CCSS.ELA-Literacy.RL.K.1 • With prompting and support, ask and answer questions about key details in a text.
CCSS.ELA-Literacy.RL.K.3 • With prompting and support, identify characters, settings, and major events in a story, using key details.
CCSS.ELA-Literacy.RL.1.5 • Explain major differences between books that tell stories and books that give information, drawing on a wide reading of a range of text types.

Social Studies Standards C-3

D2.Eco.2.K-2. Explain the benefits and costs of personal decisions.

Learning Objectives

Students will

- Recognize difference of economic needs and wants through nonfiction books and discussions.
- Compare characters, settings, and major events in two fiction books on needs and wants.
- Decide what are wants and needs on their worksheets.

Suggested Teaching Team

School library and social studies teachers.

Instructional Procedure

Lessons will be a collaborative lesson for most of the class time. Teachers are always checking for understanding. Students are more often than not involved in paired or team work so that all learners have a chance to gather ideas and be involved. Assessment is ongoing observation.

1. Teachers will read and lead discussions to compare two fiction books on needs and wants by the same author. Students will collaborate, question (inquire), collaborate and include others, and discuss and compare characters, settings, and major events in the two books. Teachers will discuss the needs outweighing the wants.

2. Teachers will discuss needs, like a shelter or house, healthy food, and clothing. They will gently explain that healthy food is a need as compared to a want. Teachers will read and discuss a nonfiction book on wants and needs. Teachers will guide the class as they inquire, curate, and examine the book illustrations to gather information on what is a want and need.

3. Students will be engaged as they color and attach the needs items to the right side of the worksheet plate and the wants will go to the left side. If time permits, they will add two more of their ideas. Their ideas will be shared.

Recommended Resources

Fiction

Boelts, Maribeth. *A Bike like Sergio's*. Somerville, MA: Candlewick, 2016.

Boelts, Maribeth. *Those Shoes*. Somerville, MA: Candlewick, 2009.

Willems, Mo. *Pigeon Needs a Bath*. New York: Hyperion. 2014.

Willems, Mo. *Pigeon Wants a Puppy*. New York, Hyperion, 2008.

Nonfiction

Bullard, Lisa. *Lily Learns about Wants and Needs*. Minneapolis, MN: Millbrook Press, 2014.

Higgins, Nadia. *Needs and Wants*. North Mankato, MN: Bullfrog Press, 2018.

Larson, Jennifer. *Do I Need It? Or Do I Want It?* Minneapolis, MN: Learner Classroom, 2010.

Olson, Gillia. *Needs and Wants*. Minneapolis, MN: Capstone, 2008

Schuh, Mari. *Wants and Needs*. Vero Beach, FL: Rourke, 2018.

Staniford, Linda. *Clothes (Wants vs Needs)*. Chicago, IL: Heinemann, 2015.

Staniford, Linda. *A Place to Live (Wants vs Needs)*. Chicago, IL: Heinemann, 2015.

Ventura, Marne. *Needs and Wants*. Minneapolis, MN: Pop!, 2018.

Waxman, Laura H. *Let's Explore Needs and Wants*. Minneapolis, MN: Lerner, 2019.

Earn Money

How Can You Earn Money?

I can help!

Earn Money, Directions

Economics: Earning money
Grade Levels Suggested: Kindergarten or Kindergarten–Second Grades

Standards

AASL Standards

AASL Standards are listed at the start of each chapter, as each of those given standards are used in each lesson, as lessons are centered on students who "inquire, include, collaborate, curate, explore, and engage" (American Association of School Librarians 2017).

Common Core Language Arts Literacy Standards

CCSS.ELA-Literacy.RL.K.3 • With prompting and support, identify characters, settings, and major events in a story, using key details of a text.

CCSS.ELA-Literacy.RL.1.5 • Explain major differences between books that tell stories and books that give information, drawing on a wide reading of a range of text types.

CCSS.ELA-Literacy.RI.K.2 • With prompting and support, identify the main topic and retell key details of a text.

Social Studies Standards C3

D2.Eco.6.K-2. Explain how people earn money.

Learning Objectives

Students will

- Identify characters and major events in a story about earning.
- Understand how one could earn through a nonfiction and a fiction book.
- Complete a worksheet on earning.

Suggested Teaching Team

School library and social studies teachers.

Instructional Procedure

Lessons will be a collaborative lesson for most of the class time. Teachers are always checking for understanding. Students are more often than not involved in paired or team work so that all learners have a chance to gather ideas and be involved. Assessment is ongoing observation.

1. Teachers will read, question, and lead discussion on the characters and major events in a fiction picture book about earning. Students will question and discuss earning as seen in the book and as related to prior knowledge.
2. Teachers will show and students will review the difference between fiction and nonfiction.
3. Teachers will read parts of a nonfiction book on earning while showing illustrations. Then students will question (inquire), include others, and discuss how earning took place. Students will include prior knowledge while problem solving and exploring the nonfiction information.
4. The class will question, discuss, and collaborate with others about how they could earn money through performing small tasks and perhaps save any money given to them.

5. Students will become engaged, as they color, cut, and paste the work they could do to earn money into the "I can help" box. Students may illustrate another work idea, if time permits.

Recommended Resources

Fiction

Bullard, Lisa, and Mike Morgan. *Ella Earns Her Own Money.* Minneapolis, MN: Millbrook Press, 2013.

Dowell, Frances O'R. *Sam the Man & the Chicken Plan.* New York: Atheneum Books, 2017.

Madson, D. L. *Money for a Puppy.* Mankato, MN: CreateSpace Independent Publishing, 2014.

Nonfiction

Buchanan, Shelly. *Earning Money.* Huntington Beach, CA: Teacher Created Materials, 2013.

Eagen, Rachel. *Learning about Earning.* New York: Crabtree Publishing, 2017.

Higgins, Nadia. *Earning Money.* North Mankato, MN: Bullfrog Books, 2018.

Larson, Jennifer S. *What Can You Do with Money?* Minneapolis, MN: Lerner, 2010.

Reynolds, Mattie. *Kids Making Money: An Introduction to Financial Literacy.* South Egremont, MA: Red Chair Press, 2013.

Waxman, Laura H.. *Let's Explore Earning Money.* Minneapolis, MN: Lerner, 2019.

Saving

Would you save your money for something? What?

Saving, Directions

Economics: Saving
Grade Levels Suggested: First Grade or Kindergarten–Second Grades

Standards

AASL Standards

AASL Standards are listed at the start of each chapter, as each of those given standards are used in each lesson, as lessons are centered on students who "inquire, include, collaborate, curate, explore, and engage" (American Association of School Librarians 2017).

Common Core Language Arts Literacy Standards

CCSS.ELA-Literacy.RL.1.5 • Explain major differences between books that tell stories and books that give information, drawing on a wide reading of a range of text types.
CCSS.ELA-Literacy.RL.1.7 • Use illustrations and details in a story to describe its characters, settings, or events.

Social Studies Standards C3

D2.Eco.2.K-2. Know the benefits and cost of personal decisions.
D2.Eco.10.K-2. Explain saving.

Learning Objectives

Students will

- Recognize the importance of saving money.
- Collaborate with others to answer questions.
- Evaluate their knowledge with worksheets' answers.
- Use illustrations and story details to describe characters, settings, and events.

Suggested Teaching Team

Math, school library, and social studies teachers.

Instructional Procedure

Lessons will be a collaborative lesson for most of the class time. Students are more often than not involved in paired or team work so that all learners have a chance to gather ideas and be involved. Assessment is ongoing observation while also checking for understanding.

1. Teachers will read a fiction picture book on saving and then lead a student discussion on author, title, characters, settings, and major events of the book. Students will also question and discuss savings as seen in the book and as related to prior knowledge.
2. Teachers will read and encourage student discussion about a nonfiction book on saving while showing the illustrations. Students will question (inquire), reflect, include and collaborate with others in the class, curate (gather information), and then discuss reflectively how to save money.
3. Teachers will lead discussion on fiction and nonfiction differences.
4. Then students will color the piggy bank given in the worksheet. Students will discuss saving. They will decide what item they would save for and circle it on their worksheets. Duplicate the piggy bank given in the worksheet and have students attach the duplicate back to the other piggy bank,

and cut out the top dark area on the pig. Students will cut out the paper coins and put them in their paper piggy banks to demonstrate saving.

Recommended Resources

Fiction

Mayer, Mercer. *Little Critter: Just Saving My Money*. New York: HarperCollins, 2010.
Rey, Hans A. *Curious George Saves His Pennies*. New York: HMH Books for Young Readers, 2014.
Roza, Greg. *A Piggy Bank for Pedro*. New York: Rosen Publishing, 2006.
Ruiz, Cecilia. *A Gift from Abuela*. Somerville, MA: Candlewick, 2018.

Nonfiction

Benjamin, Tina. *Mi Alcancia/My Piggy Bank*. Milwaukee, WI: Gareth Stevens, 2015.
Gaertner, Meg. *Spending and Saving Money*. Minneapolis, MN: Pop! 2018.
Higgins, Nadia. *Saving Money*. Minneapolis, MN: Jump!, 2018.
Schuh, Mari. *Save, Spend, or Share*. Vero Beach, FL: Rourke Educational Media, 2018.
Waxman, Laura H. *Let's Explore Saving Money*. Minneapolis, MN: Lerner, 2019.

Going for a Drink of Water

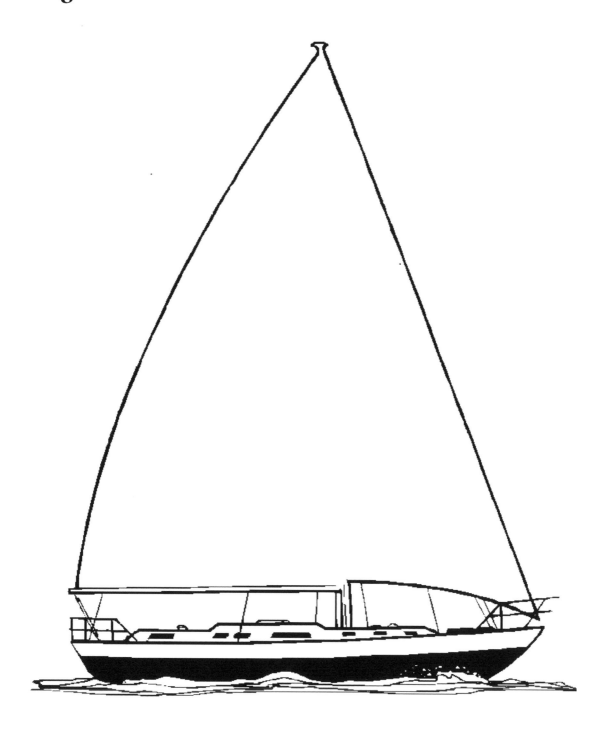

Clean water can be a scarcity. Scarcity means having much less.

On the sail, draw something to help with water scarcity.

Going for a Drink of Water, Directions

Economics: Scarcity
Grade Levels Suggested: First Grade or Kindergarten–Second Grades

Standards

AASL Standards

AASL Standards are listed at the start of each chapter, as each of those given standards are used in each lesson, as lessons are centered on students who "inquire, include, collaborate, curate, explore, and engage" (American Association of School Librarians 2017).

Common Core Language Arts Literacy Standards

CCSS.ELA-Literacy.RL.1.3 • Describe characters, settings, and major events in a story, using key details.
CCSS.ELA-Literacy.RL.1.5 • Explain major differences between books that tell stories and books that give information, drawing on a wide reading of a range of text types.
CCSS.ELA-Literacy.RL.1.7 • Use illustrations and details in a text to describe its key ideas.

Social Studies Standards C3

D2.Eco.1.K-2. Explain how scarcity makes decisions.

Learning Objectives

Students will

- Recognize scarcity.
- Realize that clean water can be scarce in the world and what can be done about the problem.
- Hear and discuss plot, character, and theme from a picture book.
- Recognize ways to have clean water from the illustrations and script given in a nonfiction book.
- Illustrate how to have clean water.

Suggested Teaching Team

School librarian and social studies teachers.

Instructional Procedure

Lessons will be a collaborative lesson for most of the class time. Students are more often than not involved in paired or team work so that all learners have a chance to gather ideas and be involved. Assessment is ongoing observation while also checking for understanding.

1. Teachers will first define *scarcity* as not having enough. Then teachers will read a fiction book about clean water.
2. Teachers will lead discussions about the plot of the story, character, and theme, including the scarcity of water.
3. Teachers will point out the differences between fiction and nonfiction books.
4. Teachers will show some illustrations and brief parts of nonfiction books about caring for water. Discussion on the scarcity of clean water in some parts of the world will be emphasized.
5. Students will collaboratively question or inquire, include and collaborate with others, curate learned knowledge, and discuss how to have enough clean water.

6. On the sail provided in the worksheet, students will reflect, take action, and become engaged in learning, by illustrating one or two ways to ensure that clean water is available.

Recommended Resources

Fiction

Kraal, Carmen L. *Hopper Needs Clean Water.* Columbia, SC: CreateSpace Independent Publishing, 2018.

Robertson, Joanne. *The Water Walker.* Toronto, ON: Second Story Press, 2017.

Senior, Olive. *Anna Carries Water.* Vancouver, BC: Tradewind Books, 2014.

Verde, Susan. *Water Princess.* New York: G. P. Putnam's Sons Books, 2016.

Walters, Eric. *Hope Springs.* Toronto, ON: Tundra Books, 2014.

Nonfiction

Bullard, Lisa. *Go Green by Caring for Water.* Minneapolis, MN: Lerner Publishing, 2018.

Bullard, Lisa. *Watch Over Our Water.* Minneapolis, MN: Millbrook Press, 2011.

Mason, Jenny. *10 Things You Can Do to Save Water.* New York: Scholastic 2017.

Minden, Cecilia. *Kids Can Keep Water Clean.* Mankato, MN: Cherry Lake Publishing, 2011.

Olien, Rebecca. *Saving Water.* North Mankato MN: Capstone, 2016.

My Bank

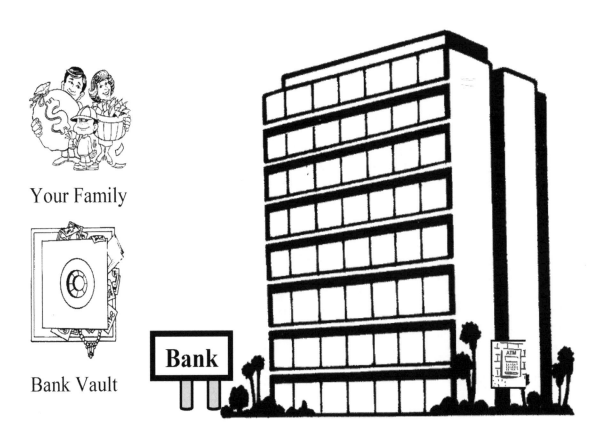

Your Family

Bank Vault

1. Draw or write how your family and you can use a bank.

2. Place the vault back in the bank. Then place your family in the bank so they can use the bank. Color it all.

My Bank, Directions

Economics: Banking
Grade Levels Suggested: Second Grade or Kindergarten–Second Grades

Standards

AASL Standards

AASL Standards are listed at the start of each chapter, as each of those given standards are used in each lesson, as they are centered on students who "inquire, include, collaborate, curate, explore, and engage" (American Association of School Librarians 2017).

Common Core Language Arts Literacy Standards

CCSS.ELA-Literacy.RL.2.1 • Ask and answer such questions as *who*, *what*, *where*, *when*, *why*, and *how* to demonstrate understanding of key details in a text.

CCSS.ELA-Literacy.RL.2.7 • Use the information gained from the illustrations and words in a print or digital text to demonstrate understanding of its characters, setting, or plot.

CCSS.ELA-Literacy. RI.2.1 • Ask and answer such questions as *who*, *what*, *where*, *when*, *why*, and *how* to demonstrate understanding of the key details in a text.

Social Studies Standards C3

D2.Eco.9.K-2. Explain the role of banks.

Learning Objectives

Students will

- Recognize the very basic role of banks for themselves and family.
- Hear and discuss a fiction book about banks while discussing characters and events.
- Use illustrations and some text to discover simple bank uses.
- Complete worksheets describing simple bank uses.

Suggested Teaching Team

School library and social studies teachers.

Instructional Procedure

Lessons will be a collaborative lesson for most of the class time. Students are more often than not involved in paired or team work so that all learners have a chance to gather ideas and be involved. Assessment is an ongoing observation while also checking for understanding.

1. Teachers will read a picture fiction book about a financial bank.
2. Students will collaboratively question and discuss how a bank was used in the story and how they and their families may use a bank through reflecting on and connecting to prior knowledge.
3. Student small groups will include and collaborate with others in order to curate or find more information about banks as nonfiction books are explored.
4. Teachers will help the class summarize the purpose of banks, including the fact that a vault keeps the money safe.

5. On their worksheets, students will choose to either illustrate or write how a bank helps. They will place the vault into the bank and place the family in the bank as if using the bank. Students will finally color their banking picture.

6. As a follow-up, students will view, discuss, interact and include with others, collaborate, and discuss a video on how banks work, as related to prior knowledge.

Recommended Resources

Fiction

Allen, Morgan. *Matthew and the Midnight Bank*. Markham, ON: Stoddart Kids, 2001.

Bulla, Lisa. *Shanti Saves Her Money*. Minneapolis, MN: Millbrook Press, 2013.

Hilbert, Margaret. *Querido Dragon Va al Banco/Dear Dragon Goes to the Bank* [Bilingual]. Chicago, IL: Norwood House, 2014.

Mayer, Mercer. *Just Saving My Money*. New York: HarperCollins, 2010.

Nonfiction

Basel, Roberta. *What Do Banks Do?* Minneapolis, MN: Capstone, 2006.

Colby, Jennifer. *Banks*. Mankato, MN: Cherry Lake Publishing, 2018.

Houghton, Gillian. *How Banks Work*. New York: PowerKids Press, 2009.

Kawa, Katie. *My First Trip to the Bank*. Milwaukee, WI: Gareth Stevens, 2012.

Larson, Jennifer S. *Where Do We Keep Money?* Minneapolis, MN: Lerner Classroom, 2010.

Northwestern Mutual. "How Banks Work." Updated 2018. http://www.themint.org/kids/how-banks-work.html.

Rau, Dana M. *What Is a Bank?* Milwaukee, WI: Gareth Stevens, 2010.

Schuh, Mari. *Money in the Bank*. Vero Beach, FL: Rourke, 2018.

Schwartz, Heather E. *Bank Wisely*. Mankato, MN: Amicus, 2016.

Goods and Services

Who Earns Money in My Community?

Match the goods or services to the community person.

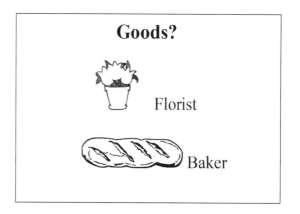

Goods?

Florist

Baker

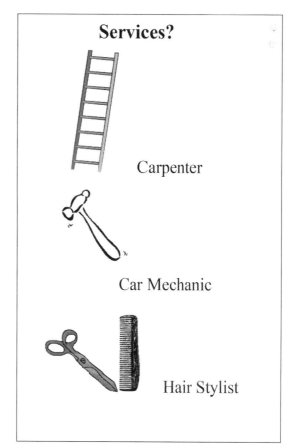

Services?

Carpenter

Car Mechanic

Hair Stylist

Who are the five other people who charge $$ for goods and services?

Goods and Services, Directions

Economics: Good and services and people earning in the community
Grade Levels Suggested: Second Grade or Kindergarten–Second Grades

Standards

AASL Standards

AASL Standards are listed at the start of each chapter, as each of those given standards are used in each lesson, as lessons are centered on students who "inquire, include, collaborate, curate, explore, and engage" (American Association of School Librarians 2017).

Common Core Language Arts Literacy Standards

CCSS.ELA-Literacy.RL.1.7 • Use illustrations and details in a text to describe its key ideas.
CCSS.ELA-Literacy.RL.2.1 • Ask and answer such questions as *who, what, where, when, why*, and *how* to demonstrate understanding of key details in a text.

Social Studies Standards C3

D2.Eco.4.K-2. Describe goods and services of local community people.
D2.Eco.6.K-2. Explain how people earn money.

Learning Objectives

Students will

- Recognize how community people earn money through goods and services.
- Define goods and services.
- Discuss how goods or services were shown in the teacher-read fiction book.
- Write the word *good* and then the word *service* on sticky notes.
- Form small groups to identify goods and services as seen in details and illustrations in nonfiction books.
- Match goods and services on their worksheets.

Suggested Teaching Team

School librarian and social studies teachers.

Instructional Procedure

Lessons will be a collaborative lesson for most of the class time. Teachers are always checking for understanding. Students are more often than not involved in paired or team work so that all learners have a chance to gather ideas and be involved. Assessment is ongoing observation.

1. Teachers will display the words *goods* and *services* on the classroom display board. Teachers will read and lead a discussion about a fiction picture book about community jobs, as related to student prior knowledge.
2. The topic of goods and services will be defined by teachers. Teachers will give examples from a nonfiction book. Students will inquire (question), include others, and discuss the definition of selling goods or services. Their results will be written on the classroom board.

3. Looking back at the first book read, students will be asked if the community jobs in the fiction picture book were about selling goods or selling services. Students will inquire and collaborate with others to get information while also problem solving the question.

4. Students will form small groups. Students in the group will write the word *goods* on three sticky notes and then write the word *services* on another three sticky notes.

5. Student small groups will examine the story details and illustrations in nonfiction books. They will question, include and collaborate with others, gather and use evidence, and discuss the illustrations in the nonfiction books in order to identify if the illustrations showed selling goods or services. Engaged students will put the sticky note on the illustrations that identified the pictures as selling a good or a service. Teachers will check for understanding.

6. Student small groups will break into pairs. Student pairs will collaborate with each other to complete the matching of goods and services to the community person, on their worksheets, as well as reflecting and answering the question.

7. The class will question, brainstorm, and discuss five other people who charge for goods or services in their community. Those names will be put on the board for students to copy for their last worksheet question.

8. Students will color their worksheets.

Recommended Resources

Fiction

Berenstain, Stan, and Jan Berenstain. *The Berenstain Bears: Jobs around Town.* Grand Rapids, MI: Zonderkids, 2011.

Clinton, Hillary R. *It Takes a Village.* New York: Simon & Schuster, 2017.

Durango, Julia. *The One Day House.* Watertown, MA: Charlesbridge, 2017.

Nonfiction

Bowman, Chris. *Construction Workers.* Brooklyn, NY: Bellwether Media, 2018.

Coan, Sharon. *Workers in My City.* Huntington Beach, CA: Teacher Created Materials, 2015.

Evans, Shira. *National Geographic Readers: Helpers in Your Neighborhood.* Washington, DC: National Geographic, 2018.

Gaerner, Meg. *Jades Trip around Town: A Book about Community Helpers.* North Mankato, MN: Child's World, 2018.

Kalman, Bobbie. *Helpers in My Community.* New York: Crabtree, 2011.

Koala, Cody. *Community Workers* [Book Set]. Minneapolis, MN: Pop!, 2019.

La Bella, Laura. *What Are Goods and Services?* Chicago, IL: Britannica Educational Publishing, 2017.

Mitten, Ellen. *Goods or Services?* Vero Beach, FL: Rourke Publishing, 2012.

Schwartz, Heather E. *Goods and Services around Town.* Huntington Beach, CA: Teacher Created Materials, 2014.

Smith, Lolo. *I Know My Community Workers.* Miami, FL: Do the Write Thing, Inc., 2018.

Frame It

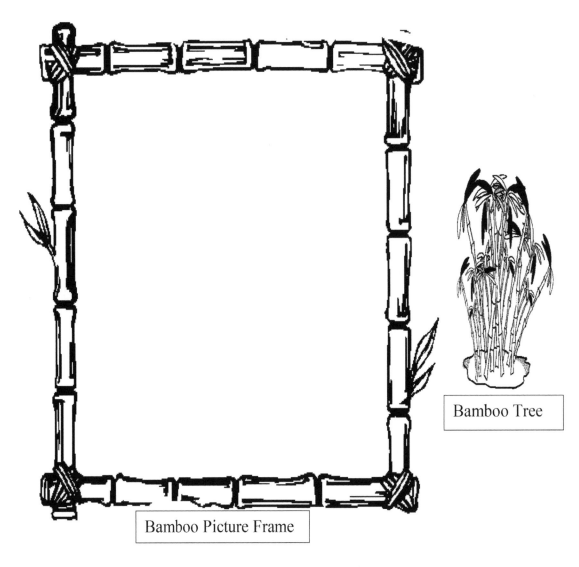

Bamboo Tree

Bamboo Picture Frame

1. Name your state: _____

2. Natural resources found in your state are_____.

3. Capital resources found in your state are _____.

4. Look at the bamboo pictures on this page.

    a) A natural resource used to make the bamboo frame is _____.

    b) Could there be a capital resource used to make the frame?   Yes   No

5. Inside the bamboo frame, create a short rhyming poem about capital and natural resources.

Frame It, Directions

Economics: Capital and natural resources
Grade Levels Suggested: Third Grade or Third–Fifth Grades

Standards

AASL Standards

AASL Standards are listed at the start of each chapter, as each of those given standards are used in each lesson, as they are centered on students who "inquire, include, collaborate, curate, explore, and engage" (American Association of School Librarians 2017).

Common Core Language Arts Literacy Standards

CCSS.ELA-Literacy.RL.3.5 • Refer to parts of stories, dramas, and poems when writing or speaking about a text; using terms such a *chapter*, *scene*, and *stanza*, describe how each successive part builds on earlier sections.

CCSS.ELA-Literacy.RI.3.7 • Use the information gained from illustrations (e.g., maps and photographs) and the words in a text to demonstrate understanding of the text (e.g., where, when, why, and how key events occur).

Social Studies Standards C3

D2.Eco.3.3-5. Identify variety of resources like human capital, physical capital, and natural resources to make goods and services.

D2.Eco.14.K-2. Describe why people trade goods and services with other countries.

Learning Objectives

Students will

- Appreciate poetry and write a poem.
- Recognize the differences between natural and capital resources.
- View a video on natural and capital resources.
- Use information from illustrations and text.
- Locate the natural and capital resources found in their state.

Suggested Teaching Team

School librarian and social studies teachers.

Instructional Procedure

Lessons will be a collaborative lesson for most of the class time. Teachers are always checking for understanding. Students are more often than not involved in paired or team work so that all learners have a chance to gather ideas and be involved. Assessment is ongoing observation.

1. This lesson may take an additional class time to complete.
2. Teachers will explain natural resources and then read a poem on natural resources. The class will discuss the poem, relate to prior knowledge, reflect, and with the help of the teachers, define the natural resources given in the poem. Answers will be put on the classroom board.
3. Teachers will show a video or briefly discuss a nonfiction book on natural resources.

4. Teachers will explain capital resources. Capital resources could be man-made things, machinery, or tools and so on. With teacher assistance, the class will question or inquire, discuss while including others and collaborating, and then define capital resources.

5. Student groups will inquire while reflecting, collaborating, curating, or collecting information text details and illustrations about the natural and capital resources found in their state as seen in a website.

6. Student pairs or groups will answer or explore and become engaged in learning by answering worksheet questions.

7. Student pairs will reflect and write a short natural resources poem in the bamboo picture frame provided in the worksheet. Teachers will designate the poem length or have students write a haiku poem.

Recommended Resources

Nonfiction

Bauman, Amy. *Earth's Natural Resources*. Milwaukee, WI: Gareth Stevens, 2007.

Blankenship, Leeann. *What Are Community Resources?* Chicago, IL: Britannica Resources, 2017.

CCKIDS. "Resources: Welcome to the Neighborhood—Crash Course Kids #2.1." Video on Resource. Updated 2015. https://www.youtube.com/watch?v=8LfD_EKze2M.

ChildEducation. "Natural Resources of the Earth." Video. Updated 2016. https://www.youtube.com/watch?v=Qw6uXh9yM54.

Clarendon Learning. "Natural Resources." Video. Updated 2018. https://www.youtube.com/watch?v=dsTgyb_ITtk.

Kids Eg. "Natural Resources." Video. Updated 2017. https://www.youtube.com/watch?v=9WMaVVvuBDM.

Loria, Laura. *What Are Resources*. New York: Rosen, 2016.

NETSTATE. "Learn about the 50 States." http://www.netstate.com/economy/ia_economy.htm.

Prior, Jennifer. *Capital Resources and the Economy*. Huntington Beach, CA: Teacher Created Materials, 2014.

Prior, Jennifer. *Our Natural Resources*. Huntington Beach, CA: Teacher Created Materials, 2014.

Rice, William. *Our Resources*. Huntington Beach, CA: Teacher Created Materials, 2015.

Sherman, Jill. *Let's Learn about Natural Resources*. Book Set. Berkeley Heights, NJ: Enslow, 2018.

Poetry Nonfiction

Archer, Micha. *Daniel Finds a Poem*. New York: Nancy Paulsen Books, 2016.

Coombs, Kate. *Water Sings Blue*. San Francisco, CA: Chronicle Books, 2012.

Davies, Nicola. *A First Book of the Sea*. Somerville, MA: Candlewick Press, 2018.

Davies, Nicola. *Outside Your Window: A First Book of Nature*. Somerville, MA: Candlewick, 2012.

Florian, Douglas. *Poetrees*. San Diego, CA: Beach Lane Books, 2010.

Krommes, Beth. *The Barefoot Book of Earth Poems*. Cambridge, MA: Barefoot Books, 2016.

Lewis, Patrick J. *National Geographic Book of Nature Poetry: More Than 200 Poems with Photographs That Float, Zoom, and Bloom!* Washington, DC: National Geographic, 2015.

Randolph, Joanne, ed. *Poems about Nature*. Holland, OH: Windmill Books, 2018.

Walker, Sally M. *Earth Verse: Haiku from the Ground Up*. Somerville, MA: Candlewick, 2018.

Apples Are Apples?

1. What is supply?

2. What is demand?

Think about supply and demand.

Next, read about apple sales and answer the following questions.

Blake was selling great apples. He had many apples. He started to sell many apples, but then Ava wanted to sell apples too.

Ava decided to sell great apples too. She had many apples too, but Ava sold her apples at a lower price.

Katie and Allie decided to sell apples too. They sold caramel apples. They did not have many. Their caramel apples had the highest price. Their apples were popular.

3. Who do you think sold all of their apples? Why?

4. How would you sell apples to make money?

5. What does supply and demand have to do with those students selling apples?

Apples Are Apples, Directions

Economics: Supply and demand
Grade Levels Suggested: Third Grade or Third–Fourth Grades

Standards

AASL Standards

AASL Standards are listed at the start of each chapter, as each of those given standards are used in each lesson, as they are centered on students who "inquire, include, collaborate, curate, explore, and engage" (American Association of School Librarians 2017).

Common Core Language Arts Literacy Standards

CCSS.ElA-Literacy.RI.3.1 • Ask and answer questions to demonstrate understanding of a text, referring explicitly to the text as the basis for the answers.
CCSS.ELA-Literacy.RI.3.7 • Use the information gained from illustrations (e.g., maps and photographs) and the words in a text to demonstrate understanding of the text (e.g., where, when, why, and how key events occur).

Social Studies Standards C3

D2.Eco.1.3-5. Know the positive and negative costs of choices.
D2.Eco.1.K-2. Explain how scarcity makes decisions.

Learning Objectives

Students will

- Understand and explain supply and demand.
- Question, evaluate, and discuss information on supply and demand.
- Collaborate with others when applying supply and demand.
- Research illustrations and text for information.

Suggested Teaching Team

Math, library, and social studies teachers.

Instructional Procedure

Lessons will be a collaborative lesson for most of the class time. Students are more often than not involved in paired or team work so that all learners have a chance to gather ideas and be involved. Assessment is ongoing observation while also checking for understanding.

1. Teachers will read a picture book on business and then lead a class discussion on supply and demand in relationship to the book and as related to student prior knowledge.
2. Student groups will be given nonfiction books on supply and demand in order for the groups to question (inquire), explore, include and collaborate with others, and curate or gather information from text details and illustrations from reading or exploring supply and demand.
3. Student groups will be engaged, as they solve the supply and demand questions mentioned in the worksheet.

Recommended Resources

Fiction

Berenstain, Mike. *The Berenstain Bear's Lemonade Stand.* New York: HarperCollins, 2014.

Blair, Shelia. *Isabel's Car Wash.* Park Ridge, IL: Albert Whitman & Company, 2008.

Kim, Ran J. *Grandpa Max's Wurst.* Los Angeles, CA: TanTan Publishing, 2017.

London, Jonathan. *Froggy's Lemonade Stand.* New York: Penguin, 2018

Parish, Herman. *Amelia Bedelia Means Business.* Saint Louis, MO: Turtleback, 2013.

Nonfiction

Adil, Janeen. *Supply and Demand.* Minneapolis, MN: Capstone, 2006.

Brennan, Linda C. *Supply and Demand.* North Mankato, MN: Child's World, 2012.

Gare, Thompson. *What Is Supply and Demand?* New York: Crabtree, 2010.

La Bella, Laura. *What Are Supply and Demand?* Chicago, IL: Britannica Educational Publishing, 2017.

Lustad, Marcia A. *Supply and Demand.* New York: Rosen, 2018.

Randolph, Ryan P. *The Price You Pay: A Look at Supply and Demand.* New York: Rosen, 2009.

Ventura, Marne. *Supply and Demand.* Minneapolis, MN: Pop!, 2019.

Sharing—Global Trade

Sharing with the World

1. Import is _____

_____ .

2. Export is _____

_____ .

3. Why do countries trade food or other things with each other? _____

_____

4. Each U.S. state trades. In the following box, illustrate one thing that your state *exports*.

Your State Export

5. In each of the following boxes, illustrate one or two foods or products that are *imported* into the United States.

U.S. Import	U.S. Import

U.S. Import	U.S. Import

From *New Standards-Based Lessons for the Busy Elementary School Librarian: Social Studies* by Joyce Keeling. Santa Barbara, CA: Libraries Unlimited. Copyright © 2020.

Sharing—Global Trade, Directions

Economics: **Global trade, a state export, and U.S. imports**
Grade Levels Suggested: Fourth Grade or Fourth–Fifth Grades

Standards

AASL Standards

AASL Standards are listed at the start of each chapter, as each of those given standards are used in each lesson, as they are centered on students who "inquire, include, collaborate, curate, explore, and engage" (American Association of School Librarians 2017).

Common Core Language Arts Literacy Standards

CCSS.ELA.RL.4.2 • Determine a theme of a story, drama, or poem from details in the text; summarize the text.

CCSS.ELA-Literacy.RI.4.7 • Interpret the information presented visually, orally, or quantitatively (e.g., in charts, graphs, diagrams, timelines, animations, or interactive elements on web pages), and explain how the information contributes to an understanding of the text in which it appears.

CCSS.ELA.RL.4.9 • Describe in depth a character, a setting, or an event in a story or drama, drawing on specific details in the text (e.g., a character's thoughts, words, or actions).

Social Studies Standards C3

D2.Eco.14.K-2. Describe why people trade goods and services with other countries.

Learning Objectives

Students will

- Recognize the differences between import and export.
- Recognize the term *global trade*.
- Understand why countries trade.
- Discuss fiction and then nonfiction sources on imports and exports.
- Use visual information.
- Describe character, setting, theme, and events.
- Locate their state exports and then the country imports while working in groups.

Suggested Teaching Team

School library and social studies teachers.

Instructional Procedures

Lessons will be a collaborative lesson for most of the class time. Teachers are always checking for understanding. Students are more often than not involved in paired or team work so that all learners have a chance to gather ideas and be involved. Assessment is ongoing observation while also checking for understanding.

1. Teachers will briefly explain export, import, and global trade by explaining that the shoes and jeans students wear could have come from another country, as well as the chocolate or coffee people enjoy.

2. Teachers will create student interest by reading and discussing a fiction picture book about trade. The class will question, reflect, and collaborate with others as they discuss an export and import theme, character, and setting as related to the story, as well as the events of the story.

3. With the guidance of teachers, student groups will examine one nonfiction book and one or two internet sites to curate, explore, and gather more information about imports and exports in order to answer their worksheet questions. If needed, students may illustrate instead of writing all worksheet answers.

4. From their research or exploration, students will become engaged learners as they illustrate and then cut out their state's export and several U.S. exports found within the boxes on the worksheet. The cut-out boxes will be used for a fun trade.

5. Trade! This will be like a trading game. Students will cut out the imported and exported boxes. Students at tables will trade products or foods with each other's products and foods in order to learn the concept of trade.

6. The class will discuss the benefits of countries trading foods or products.

7. A follow-up lesson includes viewing and discussing a video on imports and exports and then scarcity.

Recommended Resources

Fiction

Fullerton, Alma. *A Good Trade*. Toronto, ON: Pajama Press, 2013.

Yonezu, Yusuke. *A Cup for Everyone*. New York: Minedition, 2008.

Nonfiction

Andrews, Carolyn. *What Is Importing and Exporting*? Logan, IA: Perfection Learning, 2010.

Andrews, Carolyn. *What Is Trade?* New York: Crabtree, 2008.

Aurora, Jophiel. "List of Foods Imported into the U.S." Updated 2018. https://classroom.synonym.com/list-of-foods-imported-into-the-us-12080392.html.

The Balance. "U.S. Imports and Exports with Components and Statistics." https://www.thebalance.com/u-s-imports-and-exports-components-and-statistics-3306270.

Cunningham, Kevin. *Cell Phones (21st Century Skills Library: Global Products)*. Mankato, MN: Cherry Lake, 2014.

Cunningham, Kevin. *Toys (21st Century Skills Library: Global Products)*. Mankato, MN: Cherry Lake, 2014.

Eagen, Rachel. *Trade in Global Community*. New York: Crabtree, 2019.

Green, Robert. *Cars (21st Century Skills Library: Global Products)*. Mankato, MN: Cherry Lake, 2008.

Hunter, David. "Import and Export." Video. Updated 2012. https://www.youtube.com/watch?v=YMQesjJg7Rs.

Insider. "The Top Export and Import in Every US State." Updated 2018. https://www.businessinsider.com/the-top-export-and-import-in-every-us-state-2015-5.

International Trade Administration. "State Reports." Updated 2018. https://www.trade.gov/mas/ian/statereports/index.asp.

Masters, Nancy R. *Jeans (21st Century Skills Library: Global Products)*. Mankato, MN: Cherry Lake, 2014.

Meachem, Dana R. *Athletic Shoes (21st Century Skills Library: Global Products)*. Mankato, MN: Cherry Lake, 2014.

Roome, Hugh. *The Global Economy. America and the World*. New York: Children's Press, 2009.

Charge It!

Credit Card

4541 432 3343

_____
Sign your name above

A credit card is a way to borrow money. You *must* pay it back.

1. How would you describe a credit card? _____

_____

_____

_____

2. Explain interest with a credit card. _____

_____

_____

_____

3. Are you ready to get the credit card? Sign your name on the
   card on this sheet.

4. Go shopping with your credit card. Buy a book for $20.00.
   Do not forget to add a possible interest cost of $1.00.

5. Name a safety tip for using a credit card.

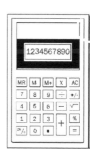

From *New Standards-Based Lessons for the Busy Elementary School Librarian: Social Studies* by Joyce Keeling.
Santa Barbara, CA: Libraries Unlimited. Copyright © 2020.

Charge It!, Directions

Economics: Credit card and interest
Grade Levels Suggested: Fourth Grade or Fourth–Fifth Grades

Standards

AASL Standards

AASL Standards are listed at the start of each chapter, as each of those given standards are used in each lesson, as they are centered on students who "inquire, include, collaborate, curate, explore, and engage" (American Association of School Librarians 2017).

Common Core Language Arts Literacy Standards

CCSS.ELA-Literacy.RL.4.1 • Refer to details and examples in a text when explaining what the text says explicitly and when drawing inferences from the text.

CCSS.ELA-Literacy.RI.4.7 • Interpret the information presented visually, orally, or quantitatively (e.g., in charts, graphs, diagrams, timelines, animations, or interactive elements on web pages), and explain how the information contributes to an understanding of the text in which it appears.

Social Studies Standards C3

D2.Eco.1.3-5. Know the positive and negative costs of choices.
D2.Eco.10.3-5. Explain interest rates.

Learning Objectives

Students will

- Recognize and define credit cards and interest.
- Research credit cards and credit card interest in small groups using nonfiction resources, referring to text visuals and details.
- Complete their worksheet and share that information with the class.

Suggested Teaching Team

School library and social studies teachers.

Instructional Procedure

Lessons will be a collaborative lesson for most of the class time. Students are more often than not involved in paired or team work so that all learners have a chance to gather ideas and be involved. Assessment is ongoing observation.

1. Students will question, discuss, and collaboratively decide how to define a credit card, as also related to prior knowledge.
2. Teachers will review an online source or lightly skim a nonfiction source on credit cards.
3. With the illustrations and text details in nonfiction books, small student groups will question (inquire) and include and collaborate with others as they discuss, curate, and explore the worksheet problems as they collectively reflect, write, and explain interest and the credit card description.
4. Small groups will then break down into student pairs in a collaborative effort to answer the rest of the worksheet.

5. Students will share their research evidence with the class and thus show engaging learning.

6. If time permits, students will hear and discuss a fiction picture book on loans or borrowing. The book will be related to credit cards.

Recommended Resources

Fiction

Bullard, Lisa. *Brody Borrows Money*. Minneapolis, MN: Millbrook Press, 2014.

Edelman, Ric. *The Squirrel Manifesto*. New York: Aladdin, 2018.

Milway, Katie S. *One Hen: How One Small Loan Made a Big Difference*. Toronto, CA: Kids Can Press, 2008.

Nonfiction

Basel, Roberta. *Checks, Credit, and Debit Cards*. Minneapolis, MN: Capstone Press, 2006.

Colby, Jennifer. *Borrowing and Returning*. Mankato, MN: Cherry Lake Publishing, 2018.

Hougton, Gillian. *How Credit Cards Work*. New York: PowerKids Press, 2009.

Minden, Cecilia. *Using Credit Wisely*. Mankato, MN: Cherry Lake Publishing, 2007.

Mooney, Carla. *Understanding Credit*. Minneapolis, MN: Lerner, 2015.

Randolph, Ryan P. *How to Use Credit*. New York: PowerKids Press, 2013.

Wells Fargo. "Hands on Banking. Credit Cards and Loans." Updated 2018. https://handsonbanking.org/kids/credit-and-you/credit-cards-loans/credit-cards-and-loans/.

Shake on It!

People often shake hands on an agreement. People like colonists and other people today agree to barter or trade services or products in exchange for something agreed to or wanted. Trading may not always be fair.

Research the following two questions:

1. List or draw two or more things that colonists traded or bartered.

If you used a book for your research, write the book title and author here:

If you used a website for your research, write the address here:

2. Not everyone shows fairness for something traded or bartered. List or draw two interesting facts about fair trade.

If you used a book for your research, write book title and author here:

If you used a website for your research, write the address here:

3. Design a tag for being fair when trading.

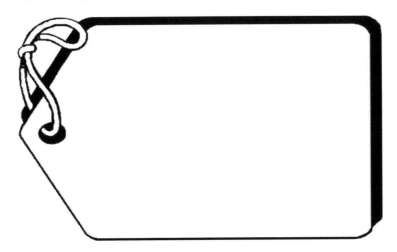

Shake on It!, Directions

Economics: Bartering and fair trade
Grade Levels Suggested: Fifth Grade

Standards

AASL Standards

AASL Standards are listed at the start of each chapter, as each of those given standards are used in each lesson, as they are centered on students who "inquire, include, collaborate, curate, explore, and engage" (American Association of School Librarians 2017).

Common Core Language Arts Literacy Standards

CCSS.ELA-Literacy.RI.5.7 • Draw on the information from multiple print or digital sources, demonstrating the ability to locate an answer to a question quickly or to solve a problem efficiently.

Social Studies Standards C3

D2.Eco.1.3-5. Know the positive and negative costs of choices.
D2.Civ.10.3-5. Identify beliefs, experiences, outlook, and values of own and others' views on civic issues.

Learning Objectives

Students will

- Recognize the concept of bartering or trading.
- Recognize bartering or trading in colonial days and today, for goods and services.
- Recognize fair trade when bartering or trading for goods and services.
- Research multiple sources, and complete their worksheets.
- Recognize and record title and author.
- Create a price tag to show fair trade.

Suggested Teaching Team

School library and social studies teachers.

Instructional Procedure

Lessons will be a collaborative lesson for most of the class time. Teachers are always checking for understanding. Students are more often than not involved in paired or team work so that all learners have a chance to gather ideas and be involved. Assessment is ongoing observation while also checking for understanding.

1. Teachers will first define bartering or trading and then help students brainstorm some products or foods that could have been bartered or traded in colonist times.
2. Teachers will ask why bartering was done in colonial times. Possible ideas could be running out of money, shortage of things, and so on.
3. Student groups will very briefly build on those ideas by connecting to prior knowledge and reflection; then inquire, include, and collaborate with others; and curate or gather information in order to answer their worksheet questions. They will first add three more ideas of foods and goods that were bartered in exchange for goods and services in colonial times on their worksheets. Students will need to record their book title and author or the website address used to find their answer.

4. Teachers will inquire if bartering was always fair in colonial times and if bartering could be fair even now. Teachers will introduce the concept of fair trade for goods and services in a simple way and perhaps as simply put as being treated fairly with fair pay and fair work conditions.

5. Students will use multiple resources. Then, small groups will do research and will locate and record information for the second question. Students will need to record their book title and author or the website address used to find their answer.

6. Student groups will have researched, recorded their information, and then share their first two worksheet answers with the class in order to show more engagement.

7. Finally, students will design a price tag to show "good" fair trade. After designing it, students may cut out the tag and attach it to lanyards or folders.

Recommended Resources

Nonfiction

Adler, David A. *Money Madness*. New York: Holiday House, 2009.

Barden, Cindy. *Life in the Colonies*. Quincy, IL: Mark Twain Media, 2001.

Brennan, Linda C. *Bartering*. North Mankato, MN: Child's World, 2014.

Faulkner, Nicholas, and Paula Johanson. *Fair Trade and You*. New York: Rosen, 2018.

Greathead, Helen. *My Chocolate Bar*. New York: Crabtree, 2016.

Greathead, Helen. *My T-Shirt and Other Clothing*. New York: Crabtree, 2016

Loewen, Nancy, and Brian Jensen. *Let's Trade: A Book about Bartering*. Mankato, MN: Picture Window Books, 2005.

National Geographic. "Colonial Trade Routes and Goods." https://www.nationalgeographic.org/photo/colonial-trade/.

Powell, Jillian. *Fair Trade*. London, UK: Wayland, 2014.

Teacher Created Materials. *Money and Trade in Our World*. Huntington Beach, CA: Teacher Created Materials, 2013.

"Trade in the Colonies." https://www.landofthebrave.info/trade-in-the-colonies.htm.

Hear All about It

Time for Taxes

				7		2				
1										
		8								
3										
					4					
9				10						
			5							
		11								
								12		
					6					

The colonists did not like paying taxes. Fill in the puzzle's white boxes for federal, state, and local governments who charge taxes for some benefits and more.

Across: (1) colonists did not like (2) who protects (3) your town is in a _____ (4) place to learn (5) air force, army, marines, and navy (6) taxes are legal _____.

Down: (2) places to swim (7) taxes charged when you buy things (8) playground (9) U.S. government (10) cars driven here (11) your town has a _____ government (12) work.

Hear All about It, Directions

Economics: Taxes in colonial times as related to now
Grade Levels Suggested: Fifth Grade

Standards

AASL Standards

AASL Standards are listed at the start of each chapter, as each of those given standards are used in each lesson, as they are centered on students who "inquire, include, collaborate, curate, explore, and engage" (American Association of School Librarians 2017).

Common Core Language Arts Literacy Standards

CCSS.ELA-Literacy.RI.5.7 • Draw on the information from multiple print or digital sources, demonstrating the ability to locate an answer to a question quickly or to solve a problem efficiently.
CCSS.ELA-Literacy.R.I.5.9 • Integrate the information from several texts on the same topic in order to write or speak about the subject knowledgeably.

Social Studies Standards C3

D2.Eco.12.3-5. Explain the ways that government pays for the goods and services it gives.

Learning Objectives

Students will

- Recognize the purposes of taxes.
- Research using multiple sources, evaluate, collaborate, and apply purposes of taxes from federal, state, and local sources.
- Complete and discuss a crossword puzzle to conclude tax purposes.

Suggested Teaching Team

Math, school librarian, and social studies teachers.

Instructional Procedure

Lessons will be a collaborative lesson for most of the class time. Teachers are always checking for understanding. Students are more often than not involved in paired or team work so that all learners have a chance to gather ideas and be involved. Assessment is ongoing observation while also checking for understanding.

1. To set the learning stage, teachers will explain a very brief history of the purpose and results of the colonial Stamp Act. A suggested source is the book by Gondosch and Cook.
2. Teachers will give a brief overview of the purposes behind taxes today, like taxes help to support public libraries, swimming pools, highways, parks, fire department, police, and more. Teachers will mention that the federal (U.S. government), state, and local governments charge taxes for things bought, for income from jobs, and for owning land.
3. Using nonfiction books or online multiple sources, student groups will inquire (question), connect to prior knowledge, reflect, include others in the group, collaborate, briefly curate or briefly research, and explore for four to five minutes to see how each of the federal, state, and local governments use taxes.

4. Students will share their research results with the class and so evaluate their results.

5. Engaged student groups will complete the crossword puzzle, answering in the numbered white boxes. There is a 2 across and a 2 down. On the board or with a projection device, teachers will display the words needed for the crossword puzzle (crossword puzzle key):

    Across: Taxes, police, state, school, military, laws

    Down: Parks, sales, pools, federal, local, highway, jobs

6. Students will discuss and reflect with their completed answers.

7. For a future lesson, students will discuss sales taxes and the percentage for their state, or the taxes taken out of paychecks. Note the resources given for this future lesson.

Recommend Resources

Nonfiction

Bedesky, Baron. *What Are Taxes?* New York: Crabtree, 2008.

Brennan, Linda C. *Taxes.* North Mankato, MN: Child's World, 2012.

Cook, Peter. *You Wouldn't Want to Be at the Boston Tea Party.* Danbury, CT: Franklin Watts, 2013.

De Capua, Sarah. *Paying Taxes.* Chicago, IL: Children's Press, 2012.

Ducksters. "Taxes." https://www.ducksters.com/history/us_government.php.

Gondosch, Linda. *How Did Tea and Taxes Spark a Revolution?* Minneapolis, MN: Lerner, 2010.

Study.com. "What Is Tax? Lesson for Kids." Updated 2018. https://study.com/academy/lesson/what-is-tax-lesson-for-kids.html.

Ventura, Marne. *Government and Community.* Minneapolis, MN: Pop!, 2018.

Resources for a Future Lesson on Taxes

The following source is a good place for students to discuss how much is taken out of checks and why:

Bix Kids. "Young Entrepreneurs: Life Guards." Updated 2018. http://bizkids.com/clip/life-guards.

The following source shows the sales tax rate:

Tax Foundation. "State and Local Tax Rates in 2016." Updated 2018. https://taxfoundation.org/state-and-local-sales-tax-rates-2016.

Chapter 3

School Library and Social Studies Teachers with Geography

This chapter covers topics of geography from Social Studies Standards, along with library literacy standards and language arts standards. The teacher librarians partner with the elementary social studies teachers to provide excellence in education with engaging lessons, with library resources and online resources, as students collaborate with others in order to create learning for all. Lessons are approximately twenty minutes long and packed with resources and based on learning standards.

The educator may apply standards that apply in their local situation if those stated are not applicable. Likewise, the educator can pick and choose from any of the three sets of standards stated—the library standards for learners, Social Studies Standards, and language arts/literacy standards—or use all of those standards as noted in each lesson. The mixture of social studies, language arts/literacy, and library or literacy skills and resources provides well-rounded opportunities for successful learning.

This chapter begins with lessons for kindergarten, with those lessons being usable for other lower elementary grades, and then the lessons move upward to the fifth grade. Grade levels are not narrowly assigned per lesson but are suggested. Furthermore, this book not only engages all learners but also offers lessons that can be intermingled for other elementary grades. There are many resources that have been tested before being suggested with each lesson, offering more teaching opportunities.

Standards

AASL Standards Framework

AASL Standards Framework for Learners

AASL Standards for Learners are listed at the start of each chapter, as each of those given standards are used in each lesson, as they are centered on students who "inquire, include, collaborate, curate, explore, and engage."

American Association of School Librarians. "AASL Standards Framework for Learners." Updated 2017. https://standards.aasl.org/framework.

AASL Standards Framework for Learners encourage learners to

1. Inquire through such means as questioning, using evidence, connecting to prior knowledge, making decisions, and more.

2. Include through such means as discussing, examining other's views, reflecting, and more.

3. Collaborate through participating, obtaining feedback, solving problems with others to connect shared learning, and more.

4. Curate through such means as determining a need and then gathering and organizing information from a variety of accurate resources, reflecting, and more.

5. Explore through such means as reading, writing, creating, asking questions, solving problems, expressing being curious, reflecting, and more.

6. Engage through such means as applying and evaluating information and sources to learning in an ethical way, including avoiding plagiarism and more.

Excerpted and adapted from *National School Library Standards for Learners, School Librarians, and School Libraries* by the American Association of School Librarians, a division of the American Library Association, copyright © 2018 American Library Association. Available for download at https://standards.aasl.org/framework. Used with permission.

Social Studies Standards—the Inquiry Arc of the C3 (College, Career, and Civic Life) Framework

Geography K-2
D2.Geo.3.K-2. Use maps, globes, and other such geographic models to identify cultural and environmental places.

D2.Geo.4.K-2. Discuss the effects of weather, climate, and other such things that affect lives in a place.

D2.Geo.1.3-5. Create maps and other graphical representations of both known and unknown places (This 3-4 standard is needed for K-2 too).

Geography 3-5
D2.Geo.1.3-5. Create maps and other graphical representations of both known and unknown places.

D2.Geo.2.3-5. Use maps and other images to show the relationship of places and regions and their environment.

D2.Geo.4.3-5. Describe how culture influences the way people change and adapt to their environments.

D2.Geo.8.3-5. Describe how human settlements and movements connect to location and natural resources.

National Council for the Social Studies. *Social Studies for the Next Generation: Purposes, Practices, and Implications of the College, Career, and Civic Life (C3) Framework for Social Studies State Standards.* Silver Spring, MD. 2013.

Common Core Standards—Literacy

Common Course Language Arts Literacy Standards or CCSS, which are given in the introductory standards section of the book, are seen with each lesson. These standards are too lengthy to be given here at the start of each chapter, but they are seen as needed for each lesson. For a complete look at this book's Common Core Standards in Literacy, refer to the introduction section.

Educators may prefer to intermingle other or additional standards or simply select some or all of the given standards. Each lesson holds a wealth of resources for educators to pick and choose from to support the standards-based learning and subsequently lessons. The standards are the foundation or framework of learning, but the teachers hold the key.

My Oceans in My World

A globe shows oceans and lands. Color the oceans blue. Add animals.

Name an ocean: _____

My Oceans in My World, Directions

Geography: Globes and atlas maps
Grade Levels Suggested: Kindergarten or Kindergarten–Second Grades

Standards

AASL Standards

AASL Standards are listed at the start of each chapter, as each of those given standards are used in each lesson, as they are centered on students who "inquire, include, collaborate, curate, explore, and engage" (American Association of School Librarians 2017).

Common Core Language Arts Literacy Standards

CCSS.ELA-Literacy.RL.K.3 • With prompting and support, identify characters, settings, and major events in a story, using key details.

CCSS.ELA-Literacy.RI.K.2 • With prompting and support, identify the main topic and retell key details of a text.

CCSS.ELA-Literacy.RL.K.6 • With prompting and support, name the author and illustrator of a story and define the role of each in telling the story.

CCSS.ELA-Literacy.RL.1.5 • Explain major differences between books that tell stories and books that give information, drawing on a wide reading of a range of text types.

Social Studies Standards C3

D2.Geo.3.K-2. Use maps, globes, and other such geographic models to identify cultural and environmental places.

Learning Objectives

Students will

- Recall the differences between fiction and nonfiction ocean books.
- Locate oceans on globes and maps.
- Recognize that there are different oceans.
- Name author, illustrator, characters, settings, and major events.
- Realize some basic ocean facts and some ocean animal names.
- Find and color the ocean on the worksheet globe, and add ocean animals.

Suggested Teaching Team

School library and social studies teachers.

Instructional Procedure

Lessons will be a collaborative lesson for most of the class time. Students are more often than not involved in paired or team work so that all learners have a chance to gather ideas and be involved. Assessment is ongoing observation while also checking for understanding.

1. Teachers will read a fiction book on the ocean and briefly discuss title, author, setting, major events, and characters.
2. Teachers will show the covers and just a few pages of nonfiction ocean books to compare nonfiction books to the fiction book just read. Students will be reminded of the differences between fiction and nonfiction.

3. Teachers will read and show two to three nonfiction ocean books, as students study the illustrations. Teachers will point out ocean facts with students' help. Students will point out ocean life too.

4. Students will be shown where oceans are located on the globe. They will note the differences between land and oceans; note how much larger the oceans are as compared to land, and the names of the major oceans, as they relate to learning to prior knowledge.

5. Small student groups will inquire, include and collaborate with others, and have a short time to explore the globe for ocean locations. The major ocean names will have been put on the class display board and will have been written on sticky notes and put on the globe too.

6. With teacher guidance, student pairs will collaborate and curate (gather knowledge) from nonfiction books, as they color the oceans blue on the globe provided in the worksheet, and then color and add ocean animals in the ocean.

7. In the remaining time, students will be shown a world atlas map, and they will note the oceans on those maps. Students will then have time to compare and discuss oceans on the map and on the globe, as they reflect on their prior knowledge.

Recommended Resources

Fiction

Galloway, Ruth. *Smiley Shark.* Wilton, CT: Tiger Tales, 2017.

Henson, Jim C. *Splash and Bubbles: The Greatest Treasure of All.* New York: HMH, 2018.

Lyall, Casey. *Inky's Great Escape: The Incredible (and Mostly True) of an Octopus Escape.* New York: Sterling, 2017.

Meister, Carl. *The Stranded Orca.* Minneapolis, MN: Stone Arch, 2014.

Montgomery, Sy. *Inky's Amazing Escape: How a Very Smart Octopus Found His Way Home.* New York: Simon & Shuster, 2018.

Mortensen, Lori. *If Wendell Had a Walrus.* New York: Henry Holt and Company, 2018.

Ocean, Davy. *The Boy Who Cried Shark (Shark School).* New York: Aladdin, 2015.

Nonfiction

Best, B. J. *Oceans.* New York: Cavendish Square, 2018.

DK. *Amazing Atlas (DK Amazing Pop-Up Books).* Ballwin, MO: DK Publishing, 2012.

Gaarder-Juntti, Gona, and Diane Craig. *What Lives in the Ocean?* Mankato, MN: Super Sandcastle ABDO, 2008.

Gardeski, Christina M. *All about Oceans.* Minneapolis, MN: Capstone Press, 2018.

Greve, Meg. *Maps Are Flat, Globes Are Round.* Vero Beach, FL: Rourke, 2009.

Guiberson, Brenda Z. *Ocean Life.* New York: Scholastic, 2011.

Little Experimenter. Little Experimenter Illuminated World Globe for Kids [Globe]. Brooklyn, NY: Little Experimenter, 2018.

Meyer, Cassie. *Oceans and Seas.* Chicago, IL: Heinemann, 2007.

National Geographic. *National Geographic Readers: Ocean Animals Collections.* Washington, DC: National Geographic, 2015.

National Geographic. *World Atlas.* Washington, DC: National Geographic, 2014.

National Geographic Kids. *National Geographic Kids My First Atlas of the World: A Child's First Picture Atlas.* Washington, DC: National Geographic Children's Books, 2018.

Oregon Scientific. Oregon Scientific Smart Discovery Globe [Globe]. Portland, OR: Oregon Scientific, 2018.

Pallota, Jerry. *The Sea Mammal Alphabet Book.* Watertown, MA: Charlesbridge, 2018.

Patchett, Fiona. *Under the Sea: Internet Referenced.* Holborn, UK: Usborne, 2006.

Rogers, Juniata. *Oceans of the World* [Book Set]. North Mankato, MN: The Child's World, 2019.

Romaine, Claire. *Oceans.* Milwaukee, WI: Gareth Stevens Publishing, 2018.

Shores, Erika L. *Oceans.* Minneapolis, MN: Pebble, Capstone, 2019.

Spilsbuery, Louise. *Oceans of the World* [Book Set]. Chicago, IL: Heinemann, 2015.

Szymanski, Jennifer. *National Geographic Readers: Into the Ocean.* Washington, DC: National Geographic, 2018.

Teckentrup, Britta. *Ocean: A Peek-Through Picture Book.* New York: Doubleday Books, 2019.

Bear Wants to Play

Look out your window. 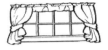 How is the weather?

Draw a hat for the bear for a snowy day. Then finish the chart.

Rain	Snow	Sun

Bear Wants to Play, Directions

Geography: Weather and its Effects
Grade Levels Suggested: Kindergarten or Kindergarten–Second Grades

Standards

AASL Standards

AASL Standards are listed at the start of each chapter, as each of those given standards are used in each lesson, as they are centered on students who "inquire, include, collaborate, curate, explore, and engage" (American Association of School Librarians 2017).

Common Core Literacy Standards

CCSS.ELA-Literacy.RL.K.3 • With prompting and support, identify characters, settings, and major events in a story, using key details.

CCSS.ELA-Literacy.RL.K.7 • With prompting and support, describe the relationship between illustrations and the story in which they appear (e.g., what moment in a story an illustration depicts).

CCSS.ELA-Literacy.RI.K.2 • With prompting and support, identify the main topic and retell key details of a text.

CCSS.ELA-Literacy.RL.1.5 • Explain major differences between books that tell stories and books that give information, drawing on a wide reading of a range of text types.

Social Studies Standards C3

D2.Geo.4.K-2. Discuss the effects of weather, climate, and other such things that affect lives in a place.

Learning Objectives

Students will

- Hear and discuss a picture fiction book about an aspect of weather.
- Discuss characters, settings, and main events.
- Discuss the differences of fiction and nonfiction.
- Discuss the nonfiction books on a rainy, snowy, and sunny day, and how it would affect them.
- Identify main topic and details of a text.
- Complete the worksheet chart on a rainy, snowy, and sunny day.

Suggested Teaching Team

School library and social studies teachers.

Instructional Procedure

Lessons will be a collaborative lesson for most of the class time. Students are more often than not involved in paired or team work so that all learners have a chance to gather ideas and be involved. Assessment is ongoing observation while also checking for understanding.

1. Teachers will introduce the lesson on weather and how it relates to students, by first reading a fiction picture book about a bear with either a rainy, snowy, or sunny day. Students will discuss character, setting, and main event. Students will question and discuss the illustrations and text in relationship to weather.

2. Teachers will remind students that fiction is not real whereby nonfiction is real. With student assistance, teachers will introduce the nonfiction weather books on a sunny, rainy, and snowy day; point out general facts and main topics; and then discuss why the information is nonfiction. By connecting to prior knowledge, students will question and discuss what to wear on a sunny, rainy, or snowy day.

3. On student worksheets, teachers will have students explain items on the worksheet so that all students will be able to identify the items for worksheet work.

4. Students will then collaborate with others, as they decide what they could draw for the bear's hat for a snowy day. Review of the books on snowy days may be briefly needed. Students will draw the stocking hat for the bear or another type of winter hat.

5. Engaged students will help each other at tables, as they inquire or question, collaborate with others, curate or organize information, and color, cut out, match, and glue the hats and then another item useful on the snowy, rainy, or sunny day, on the worksheet chart. For instance, a rainy day would need the umbrella and hat to keep off the rain. A snowy day would need the stocking hat and a sled.

6. In the remaining time, student pairs or small groups will examine the weather books and reflect on what it is like to have that kind of weather.

Recommended Resources

Fiction

Bing, Bo. *Little Bear's Sunshine*. Adelaide, Australia: Starfish Bay Children's Books, 2016.

Blackstone, Stella. *Bear in Sunshine/Oso Bajo El Sol* [Bilingual]. Cambridge, MA: Barefoot Books, 2009.

Gravett, Emily. *Bear & Hare Snow!* New York: Simon & Schuster, 2015.

Hillenbrand, Will. *Kite Day: A Bear and Mole Story*. New York: Holiday House, 2012.

Lies, Brian. *Got to Get to Bear's!* New York: Houghton Mifflin, 2018.

Make Believe Ideas LTD. *Story Book Little Bear's Big Adventure*. Nashville, TN: Thomas Nelson, 2017.

Pinder, Eric. *How to Build a Snow Bear*. New York: Farrar Straus Giroux, 2016.

Weinberger, Michael. *Oogie's Rainy Day Adventure*. New York: Purple Mountain Publishing, 2017.

Nonfiction

Appleby, Alex. *It's Rainy!* Milwaukee, WI: Gareth Stevens, 2014.

Appleby, Alex. *It's Snowing!* Milwaukee, WI: Gareth Stevens, 2014.

Appleby, Alex. *It's Sunny!* Milwaukee, WI: Gareth Stevens, 2014.

Bauer, Marion D. *Rain*. New York: Simon Spotlight, 2016.

Bauer, Marion D. *Snow*. New York: Simon Spotlight, 2016.

Bauer, Marion D. *Sun*. New York: Simon Spotlight, 2016.

Cox-Cannons, Helen. *Rain*. Chicago, IL: Heinemann, 2015.

Cox-Cannons, Helen. *Snow*. Chicago, IL: Heinemann, 2015.

Cox-Cannons, Helen. *Sunshine*. Chicago, IL: Heinemann, 2015.

Rice, Dona. *Weather Wear*. Huntington Beach, CA: Teacher Created Materials, 2019.

Rice, Dona. *What Kind of Weather*. Huntington Beach, CA: Teacher Created Materials, 2010.

Rustad, Martha E. H. *Today Is a Rainy Day*. Minneapolis, MN: Capstone, 2017.

Rustad, Martha E. H. *Today Is a Snowy Day*. Minneapolis, MN: Capstone, 2017.

Rustad, Martha E. H. *Today Is a Sunny Day*. Minneapolis, MN: Capstone, 2017.

North and South

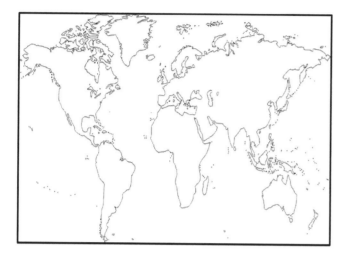

World Map

World Globe

Where is north and south?

1. On the map, draw lines to where these words go: | North | South |

2. On the globe, draw lines to where these words go: | North | South |

3. The north of the world is the North Pole. Is it cold or hot?

4. Which animal lives at the North Pole?

5. The south of the world is the South Pole. Is it cold or hot?

6. Which animal lives at the South Pole?

North and South, Directions

Geography: Globes and atlas maps—North and South Poles
Grade Levels Suggested: First Grade or First–Second Grades

Standards

AASL Standards

AASL Standards are listed at the start of each chapter, as each of those given standards are used in each lesson, as lessons are centered on students who "inquire, include, collaborate, curate, explore, and engage" (American Association of School Librarians 2017).

Common Core Language Arts Literacy Standards

CCSS.ELA-Literacy.RL.1.7 • Use illustrations and details in a story to describe its characters, settings, or events.
CCSS.ELA-Literacy.RL.1.3 • Describe characters, settings, and major events in a story, using key details.

Social Studies Standards C3

D2.Geo.4.K-2. Discuss the effects of weather, climate, and other such things that affect lives in a place.
D2.Geo.3.K-2. Use maps, globes, and other such geographic models to identify cultural and environmental places.

Learning Objectives

Students will

- Recall the differences between fiction and nonfiction books.
- Hear and discuss the character and setting/location of penguins and then polar bears from the picture fiction books and their illustrations.
- Locate and map north and south on the map and globe.
- Hear a nonfiction book on the North and South Poles, and again discuss those directions.
- Answer questions given in the worksheet.

Suggested Teaching Team

School library and social studies teachers.

Instructional Procedure

Lessons will be a student collaborative lesson for most of the class time. Teachers are always checking for understanding. Students are more often than not involved in paired or team work so that all learners have a chance to gather ideas and be involved. Assessment is ongoing observation while also checking for understanding.

1. Character and setting will be discussed as teachers read a picture fiction book on a penguin and also explain that penguins live at the South Pole and then read and discuss a picture fiction book on polar bears. Teachers will explain that polar bears are found at the North Pole.

2. Teachers will need to have the words North and South written on large slips of paper, and then refer to those words. Teachers will show students north and south on world globe and world atlas map. They will emphasize and show that the North and South Poles are very cold and are located

at the most northern and most southern part of the world. Student pairs will need to take turns inquiring, reflecting, and collaborating with each other as they discover south and north on a world globe and/or world map.

3. Teachers will skim and discuss a nonfiction book on both the South and North Poles. Illustrations will be emphasized. Teachers will ask students what they learned about the South and North Poles. Teachers will remind and show students where on the world globe the South and North Poles are located.

4. Students will inquire, connect to prior or learned knowledge, and collaborate and include with others as they solve their worksheet problems as teachers read the worksheets to them. As carefully guided by teachers, students will write the words North on the top of their papers, and then South at the bottom of the worksheet globe and map. Then, students will answer worksheet questions.

5. Finally, engaged students will reflect as they write or draw how their family would react if going to see the South Pole briefly.

6. In the remaining time, students will continue finding north and south directions on the map or globe or browse nonfiction books on penguins or polar bears.

Recommended Resources

Fiction

Andreae, Giles. *Be Brave, Little Penguin.* New York: Orchard Books, 2017.
Beer, Hans D. *The Adventures of the Little Polar Bear.* New York: North-South Books, 2018.
Bonilla, Lindsay. *Polar Bear Island.* New York: Sterling Children's Books, 2018.
Heder, Thrya. *The Bear Report.* New York: Abrams Books, 2015.
Judge, Lita. *Penguin Flies Home.* New York: Atheneum Books, 2019.
McGrath, Barbara B. *Five Flying Penguins.* Watertown, MA: Charlesbridge, 2018.
Ozley, Jennifer. *Peg + Cat: The Penguin Problem.* Somerville, MA: Candlewick, 2016.
Thomson, Sarah. *Cub's Big World.* New York: Houghton Mifflin Harcourt, 2013.

Nonfiction

Best, B. J. *Penguins.* New York: Cavendish Square, 2017.
Cooper, Katz S. *A Day in the Life of a Polar Bear.* Minneapolis, MN: Pebble, 2019.
Dinmont, Kerry. *It's a Polar Bear!* Minneapolis, MN: Bumba Books Lerner, 2019.
Gardeski, Christina M. *All about the North and South Poles (Habitats).* Minneapolis, MN: Capstone, 2017.
Gifford, Clive. *In Focus: Polar Lands.* New York: Kingfisher, 2017.
Jenner, Cary. *DK Readers L1 Frozen Worlds.* New York: DK Publishing, 2017.
Levinson, Nancy S., and Diane D. Heam. *North Pole, South Pole.* New York: Holiday House, 2002.
Little Experimenter. Little Experimenter Illuminated World Globe for Kids [Globe]. Brooklyn, NY: Little Experimenter, 2018.
National Geographic. *National Geographic Kids World Atlas.* Washington, DC: National Geographic, 2013.
National Geographic Children's Books. *National Geographic Kids World Atlas.* 5th ed. Washington, DC: National Geographic, 2018.
Oregon Scientific. Oregon Scientific Smart Discovery Globe [Globe]. Portland, OR: Oregon Scientific, 2018.
Pettiford, Rebecca. *Polar Bears.* Brunswick, MD: Bellwether Media, 2019.
Schuh, Mari. *Penguins.* Minneapolis, MN: Capstone Press, 2017.
Sill, Cathryn P. *All about Penguins.* Atlanta, GA: Peachtree, 2013.
Stass, Leo. *Penguins.* Mankato, MN: ABDO, 2017.
Worth, Bonnie. *Ice Is Nice! All about the North and South Poles.* New York: Random, 2010.

Finding Your Way in the Library

Library Map Key

Card Catalog Computers: ◯　　Tables: ▭　　Easy Books: **E**

Fiction: **F**　　Check Out Desk: 📚　　Nonfiction: 🐻

A map key helps you find things on a map. Look at the map key to answer the following:

1. There are _____ shelves in the **Easy** books.

2. There are _____ tables.

3. There are _____ nonfiction shelves.

4. There are _____ **Fiction** shelves.

Finding Your Way in the Library, Directions

Geography: Directions with a map key
Grade Levels Suggested: First Grade or First–Third Grades

Standards

AASL Standards

AASL Standards are listed at the start of each chapter, as each of those given standards are used in each lesson, as they are centered on students who "inquire, include, collaborate, curate, explore, and engage" (American Association of School Librarians 2017).

Common Core Language Arts Literacy Standards

CCSS.ELA-Literacy.RL.1.7 • Use illustrations and details in a story to describe its characters, settings, or events.

CCSS.ELA-Literacy.RI.2.1 • Ask and answer such questions as who, what, where, when, why, and how to demonstrate understanding of the key details in a text.

Social Studies Standards C3

D2.Geo.3.K-2. Use maps, globes, and other such geographic models to identify cultural and environmental places.

Learning Objectives

Students will

- Recognize a map key.
- Recognize setting.
- Hear and discuss a video or book about a map key while examining key text details.
- Complete their worksheet using a map key.

Suggested Teaching Team

School library and social studies teachers.

Instructional Procedure

Lessons will be a collaborative lesson for most of the class time. Students are more often than not involved in paired or team work so that all learners have a chance to gather ideas and be involved. Assessment is ongoing observation while also checking for understanding.

1. Teacher will show and discuss how students will use a map key for a map through books about map keys or show a video about a map key.
2. Teachers will read a humorous picture fiction book that has the library as the subject. Title, author, and setting will be discussed. As the book is being read, teacher librarians will point out different places in the library as seen in the book.
3. Teachers will point out that their school library has different places for certain books. Each book has a special place. For instance, teachers will show where a nonfiction or a book on real things is found and where easy or fiction books are found. Then teachers will point out that a map helps find things.

4. Student pairs will use the map key to find the location of certain places on their school library worksheet. Teachers will first ask students how many card catalog computers are on the worksheet library. Teachers will keep reading the questions and allowing student pairs time to collaborate and include each other and question or inquire, as they organize the information given in the worksheet, explore, and then solve their worksheet questions.

5. Students will browse children's atlases to practice using map keys.

Recommended Resources

Fiction

Becker, Bonny. *A Library Book for Bear.* Somerville, MA: Candlewick Press, 2014.

Dean, James. *Pete the Cat Checks Out the Library.* New York: HarperCollins Publishers, 2018.

Donald, Allison. *The New LiBEARian.* New York: Houghton Mifflin Harcourt, 2018.

Funk, Josh. *Lost in the Library: A Story of Patience & Fortitude.* New York: Henry Holt, 2018.

Gassman, Julie. *Do Not Bring Your Dragon to the Library.* Minneapolis, MN: Capstone, 2016.

King, M. G. *Librarian on the Roof! A True Story.* Park Ridge, IL: Albert Whitman, 2010.

Kirk, Daniel. *Library Mouse: Home Sweet Home.* New York: Abrams Books for Young Readers, 2013.

Mitchell, Malcolm. *The Magician's Hat.* New York: Scholastic, 2018.

Papp, Lisa. *Madeline Finn and the Library Dog.* Atlanta, GA: Peachtree, 2018.

St. John, Amanda. *How to Find a Book.* Alberta, CA: Weigl, 2018.

Nonfiction

Aberg, Rebecca. *Map Keys.* New York: Scholastic, 2003.

Leedy, Loreen. *Mapping Penny's World.* New York: Square Fish, 2003.

National Geographic Children's Books. *National Geographic Kids World Atlas.* 5th ed. Washington, DC: National Geographic, 2018.

Ritchie, Scot. *Follow That Map! A First Book of Mapping Skills.* Boston, MA: Kids Can Press, 2009.

Smithsonian. *Smithsonian Children's Illustrated Atlas.* New York: DK, 2016.

Sweeney, Joan. *Me on the Map.* New York: Dragonfly Books, 2018.

Taylor, Barbara. *Children's Animal Atlas.* Irving, CA: QEB, 2018.

Videos4kids.tv. "Learn about Maps—Symbols, Map Key, Compass Rose." Video. Updated 2011. https://www.youtube.com/watch?v=dp8VOG8Cgag.

My Town

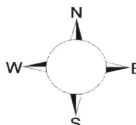

Use this compass rose to find places in your new town.

1. School is over for the day. What direction will you go to get to the park playground?

2. As you are leaving the playground, you want to get milk at the store. What direction will you go to get to the store?

3. After getting milk at the store, what direction will you go to get to your house?

4. After dinner at your house, you get to go to the movies. What direction will you go?

5. It has been a good day in your new town. Could you give directions to someone else?

My Town, Directions

Geography: Directions in "My Town," using a compass rose
Grade Levels Suggested: Second Grade or First Grade–Second Grades

Standards

AASL Standards

AASL Standards are listed at the start of each chapter, as each of those given standards are used in each lesson, as they are centered on students who "inquire, include, collaborate, curate, explore, and engage" (American Association of School Librarians 2017).

Common Core Language Arts Literacy Standards

CCSS.ELA-Literacy.RL.2.7 • Use the information gained from the illustrations and words in a print or digital text to demonstrate understanding of its characters, setting, or plot.

CCSS.ELA-Literacy.RI.2.1 • Ask and answer such questions as who, what, where, when, why, and how to demonstrate understanding of the key details in a text.

Social Studies Standards C3

D2.Geo.1.3-5. Create maps and other graphical representations of both known and unknown places.

Learning Objectives

Students will

- Recall the differences between fiction and nonfiction books.
- Hear and discuss character and setting of a fiction picture book about a town.
- Hear and discuss a book discussing a compass rose.
- Be able to describe a compass rose and know how to use it.
- Answer worksheet questions about a compass rose.

Suggested Teaching Team

School library and social studies teachers.

Instructional Procedure

Lessons will be a collaborative lesson for most of the class time. Teachers are always checking for understanding. Students are more often than not involved in paired or team work so that all learners have a chance to gather ideas and be involved. Assessment is ongoing observation while also checking for understanding.

1. Character and setting will be discussed by students, as teachers read a picture fiction book on a town or someone coming to a new town. Setting and character will be discussed.

2. Small student groups or student pairs will browse through nonfiction books for key details on a town. The main focus of this lesson is not the people in the community but what things are located in a town. Student groups will question or inquire and include and collaborate with others in the groups, as they gather the information (curate), explore, and then explain what places are found in a town, like a library, a park, and other locations.

3. Teachers will then explain that someone new to a town may not know where to find everything in town. So a town map would help. It is helpful to know how to read or use a map.

4. Teachers will explain that a compass rose helps to find things, as the compass rose has the (cardinal) direction letters that represent the directions. Teachers will need to write the cardinal direction words with each accompanying letter on the classroom display board (N = North and others) so that students will be able to spell the directions correctly for their worksheet.

5. Teachers will briefly show and discuss a book on a compass rose.

6. Teachers will explain that students will pretend to be new to a town and would not know how to find their way. Student pairs will inquire, collaborate, and explore how to use the worksheet compass rose to find their way in a "new town" on their worksheets. If desired, students may lightly fasten a paper fastener in the middle of the compass rose so that they can actually make the directions move on the compass rose. Teachers will tell students to write the direction word instead of just the cardinal direction letter on their worksheet answers.

7. When their worksheet questions are answered, student pairs will create another direction question for their town worksheet for another student pair to answer.

8. If time permits, student pairs can keep adding compass rose questions for other students to answer. They may need to label more things on the town map. This will enable students to reflect on learning and become more engaged learners.

Recommended Resources

Fiction

Bullard, Lisa. *This Is My Town*. Minneapolis, MN: Millbrook Press, 2017.
Christopher, Kevin. *Amira Can Catch, New Kid*. West Beach, FL: Clarens Publishing, 2018.
De La Pena, Matt. *Last Stop on Market Street*. New York: G.P. Putnam's Sons, 2015.
Duddle, Jonny. *The Pirates Next Door*. London, UK: Templar, 2012.
Dungy, Tony. *Maria Finds Courage*. Eugene, OR: Harvest House Publishers, 2018.
Gaetner, Meg. *Jade's Trip around Town*. North Mankato, MN: Child's World, 2019.
Kyle, Tracey. *Food Fight Fiesta! A Tale of La Tomatina*. New York: Sky Pony Press, 2018.
Verde, Susan. *Hey, Wall: A Story of Art and Community*. New York: Simon & Schuster, 2018.
Yang, Bell. *Angel in Beijing*. Somerville, MA: Candlewick, 2018.

Compass Rose Nonfiction

Besel, Jennifer M. *Compass Roses and Directions*. Minneapolis, MN: Capstone Press, 2013.
Boswell, Kelly. *Maps, Maps, Maps!* Minneapolis, MN: Capstone Press, 2014.
McAneney, Caitlin. *The Compass Rose and Cardinal Directions*. Milwaukee, WI: Gareth Stevens, 2015.
Olien, Rebecca. *Map Keys*. New York: Scholastic, 2012.
Phan, Sandy. *Getting around Town*. Huntington Beach, CA: Teacher Created Materials, 2014.

Nonfiction—General

Austen, Mary. *We Live in a Small Town*. New York: PowerKids, 2016.
Benjamin, Tina. *Donde Yo Vivo/Where I Live* [Bilingual]. Translated by Charlotte Bockman. Milwaukee, WI: Gareth Stevens, 2015.
Benjamin, Tina. *Where I Live*. Milwaukee, WI: Gareth Stevens, 2015.
Bodden, Valerie. *A Town*. Mankato, MN: Creative Education, 2009.
Kenney, Diana. *What Makes a Town?* Huntington Beach, CA: Teachers Created Materials, 2014.
McDowell, Pamela. *Small Town (AV2 Let's Read! Where Do You Live?)*. Alberta, CA: Weigel, 2018.
Summers, Portia. *Zoom in on Communities Book Set*. Berkeley Heights, NJ: Enslow Publishing, 2017.

Oceans

Oceans are large bodies of salt water. Oceans can be around an island and at the edge of other land. Do you see the ocean around the island? Do you see the dark island lake?

1. Look at the island picture. What is the biggest body of water? Ocean or lake?

2. What body of water is close to where you live? Ocean or lake?

3. Find the world oceans. Draw a line from the ocean's name to its' map place.

Pacific Ocean Atlantic Ocean Indian Ocean Artic Ocean Southern Ocean

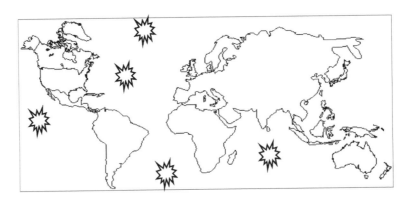

4. How does a lake or an ocean close to you make a difference for you and others?

Oceans, Directions

Geography: Globes and atlas maps
Grade Levels Suggested: Second Grade or Second–Third Grades

Standards

AASL Standards

AASL Standards are listed at the start of each chapter, as each of those given standards are used in each lesson, as they are centered on students who "inquire, include, collaborate, curate, explore, and engage" (American Association of School Librarians 2017).

Common Core Language Arts Literacy Standards

CCSS.ELA-Literacy.RL.1.5 • Explain major differences between books that tell stories and books that give information, drawing on a wide reading of a range of text types.

CCSS.ELA-Literacy.RI.2.1 • Ask and answer such questions as who, what, where, when, why, and how to demonstrate understanding of the key details in a text.

CCSS.ELA-Literacy.RL.2.7 • Use the information gained from the illustrations and words in a print or digital text to demonstrate understanding of its characters, setting, or plot.

Social Studies Standards C3

D2.Geo.1.3-5. Create maps and other graphical representations of both known and unknown places. [Will create oceans on a graphic representation]

Learning Objectives

Students will

- Recall the differences between fiction and nonfiction ocean books.
- Locate oceans on globes and maps.
- Hear and discuss a fiction picture book's illustrations and characters.
- Recognize that there are different oceans.
- Realize some basic ocean facts and some ocean animal names from key details and illustrations in nonfiction sources.
- Find and color the ocean on the worksheet globe, write down an ocean name, and add ocean animals.

Suggested Teaching Team

School library and social studies teachers.

Instructional Procedure

Lessons will be a collaborative student lesson for most of the class time. Students are more often than not involved in paired or team work so that all learners have a chance to gather ideas and be involved. Assessment is ongoing observation while also checking for understanding.

1. The major ocean names will be put on the class display board. Teachers will read a fiction picture book on the ocean and briefly discuss title, author, setting, and characters. Teachers will show the covers and just a few pages of nonfiction ocean books to compare nonfiction books to the fiction book just read. Then students will review fiction and nonfiction differences.

2. Teachers will skim and show two or three nonfiction ocean books' illustrations and key details to students. Teachers will point out ocean facts and key details. Students will point out ocean life.

3. Students will be shown the location of oceans on a globe. They will note the differences between land and oceans, how large the oceans are as compared to land, and the names of the major oceans. Groups will have a few seconds to collaboratively examine the globe for oceans.

4. Using nonfiction books, student pairs will question (inquire), collaboratively include each other, as they curate or gather information, and apply it when answering the ocean locations on the worksheet. On the worksheet, engaged students will simply draw lines from the ocean names in bold to the map locations.

5. As a class, students will discuss if they live closer to a lake or an ocean. They will brainstorm how the lake or ocean makes a difference for them or other things (animals).

6. In the remaining time, students will be shown a world atlas map and note the oceans on those maps. Students will then have time to compare and discuss oceans on the map and on the globe.

Recommended Resources

Fiction

Galloway, Ruth. *Smiley Shark.* Wilton, CT: Tiger Tales, 2017.

Henson, Jim C. *Splash and Bubbles: The Greatest Treasure of All.* New York: HMH, 2018.

Lyall, Casey. *Inky's Great Escape: The Incredible (and Mostly True) of an Octopus Escape.* New York: Sterling, 2017.

Meister, Carl. *The Stranded Orca.* Minneapolis, MN: Stone Arch, 2014.

Montgomery, Sy. *Inky's Amazing Escape: How a Very Smart Octopus Found His Way Home.* New York: Simon & Shuster, 2018.

Mortensen, Lori. *If Wendell Had a Walrus.* New York: Henry Holt and Company, 2018.

Ocean, Davy. *The Boy Who Cried Shark (Shark School).* New York: Aladdin, 2015.

Nonfiction

Best, B. J. *Oceans.* New York: Cavendish Square, 2018.

Gardeski, Christina M. *All about Oceans.* Minneapolis, MN: Capstone Press, 2018.

Greve, Meg. *Maps Are Flat, Globes Are Round.* Vero Beach, FL: Rourke, 2009.

Guiberson, Brenda Z. *Ocean Life.* New York: Scholastic, 2011.

Little Experimenter. Little Experimenter Illuminated World Globe for Kids [Globe]. Brooklyn, NY: Little Experimenter, 2018.

National Geographic. *National Geographic Readers: Ocean Animals Collections.* Washington, DC: National Geographic, 2015.

National Geographic. *National Geographic World Atlas.* Washington, DC: National Geographic, 2014.

National Geographic Kids. *National Geographic Kids My First Atlas of the World: A Child's First Picture Atlas.* Washington, DC: National Geographic Children's Books, 2018.

Oregon Scientific. Oregon Scientific Smart Discovery Globe [Globe]. Portland, OR: Oregon Scientific, 2018.

Pallota, Jerry. *The Sea Mammal Alphabet Book.* Watertown, MA: Charlesbridge, 2018.

Rogers, Juniata. *Oceans of the World* [Book Set]. North Mankato, MN: The Child's World, 2019.

Romaine, Claire. *Oceans.* Milwaukee, WI: Gareth Stevens Publishing, 2018.

Shores, Erika L. *Oceans.* Minneapolis, MN: Pebble, Capstone, 2019.

Spilsbuery, Louise. *Oceans of the World* [Book Set]. Chicago, IL: Heinemann, 2015.

Szymanski, Jennifer. *National Geographic Readers: Into the Ocean.* Washington, DC: National Geographic Children's Books, 2018.

My State Landforms

1. What is a landform? _____

_____

_____

2. List eight to ten landforms: _____

_____

_____

3. Make a colorful small poster advertising the wonderful landforms that a person would see in your state. Colorfully write your state name. Draw and label two to three landforms found in your state.

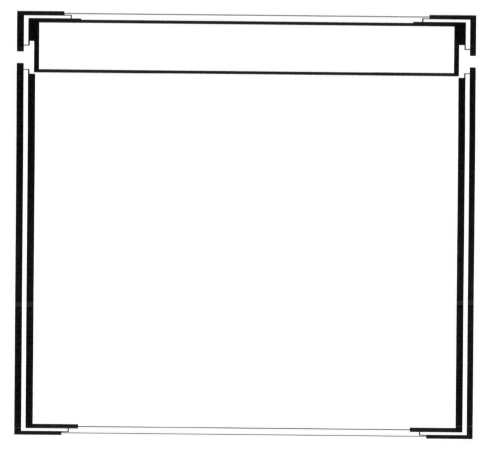

My State Landforms, Directions

Geography: Landforms, landforms and my state
Grade Levels Suggested: Third Grade or Third–Fifth Grades

Standards

AASL Standards

AASL Standards are listed at the start of each chapter, as each of those given standards are used in each lesson, as lessons are centered on students who "inquire, include, collaborate, curate, explore, and engage" (American Association of School Librarians 2017).

Common Core Language Arts Literacy Standards

CCSS.ElA-Literacy.RI.3.1 • Ask and answer questions to demonstrate understanding of a text, referring explicitly to the text for answers.
CCSS.ELA-Literacy.RI.3.7 • Use the information gained from illustrations (e.g., maps and photographs) and the words in a text to demonstrate understanding of the text (e.g., where, when, why, and how key events occur).

Social Studies Standards C3

D2.Geo.8.3-5. Describe how human settlements and movements connect to location and natural resources.

Learning Objectives

Students will

- View and discuss the video about landforms and the visuals.
- Define *landforms* and give examples.
- Answer worksheet questions on landforms from the information given in written form in texts and the information given in illustrations in the text.
- Create a mini poster advertising their state landforms.
- Hear and discuss a funny poem about a vacation, if time permits.

Suggested Teaching Team

School library and social studies teachers.

Instructional Procedure

Lessons will be a collaborative lesson for most of the class time. Students are more often than not involved in paired or team work so that all learners have a chance to gather ideas and be involved. Assessment is ongoing observation while also checking for understanding.

Note: National Geographic (2018) defines a *landform* as "A landform [that] is a feature on the Earth's surface that is part of the terrain. Mountains, hills, plateaus, and plains are the four major types of landforms." So the top of the worksheet shows a mountain, plateau, plain, and hill. A cave is also included. A good resource to show and discuss landforms are the books on national parks. The "World Atlas" site also shows landforms for each state.

1. This lesson will take two sessions. Teachers will introduce the landforms lesson by showing a video about landforms. Students will then collaboratively and collectively define a *landform* as exemplified in the video visuals and give some examples. Second, discussion will include how a

landform could affect where people live and build their communities. Finally, teachers will briefly mention that landforms affect not only where people live but also where people would go on vacation.

2. Small student groups will question, include all when gathering information (curate), and explore different landform nonfiction books and look for facts from the books' illustrations. After three to four minutes, engaged student groups will share only the new important facts they have found.

3. Small groups will answer the top two questions given in the worksheet.

4. Teachers will remind students that people would go on vacations to see landforms in different states. Small groups will question, collaborate, gather information, explore and reflect, and locate landforms that can be found in their state through using a national parks book or a geographic atlas. The last recommended reference on the list shows landforms for each state.

5. After research, student pairs will create a colorful mini poster advertising their state landforms for a vacation destination. The top box of the poster will have the name of the state neatly but colorfully written.

6. Student pairs will colorfully but neatly draw and then label two or three of their state landforms on the poster. Students should include a small outline of their state. If desired, students could include more tourist attraction landforms of their state. Posters will be displayed.

7. If time permits, a humorous poem on taking a trip could be read.

Recommended Resources

Nonfiction

Birt, Caroline. "Kids Geology. Landforms." Updated 2015. https://kidsgeo.com/geology-for-kids/landforms/.

Brennan, Linda C. *U.S. Landforms: What You Need to Know.* Minneapolis, MN: Capstone, 2018.

DeMaio. "Learning about Landforms." Video. Updated, 2013. https://www.youtube.com/watch?v=KWTDmg8OI_Y.

Fodor. *The Official Guide to America's National Parks.* New York: Fodor/Random, 2012.

Green, John, and Hank Green. "Landforms, Hey! Crash Course Juds #17.1." Video. Updated 2015. https://www.youtube.com/watch?v=FN6QX43QB4g.

Haskell, J. P. *Earth's Many Landforms.* New York: Rosen, 2013.

Kalman, Bobbie. *What Are Landforms?* New York: Crabtree, 2018.

Lindeen, Mary. *Landforms.* Chicago, IL: Norwood House Press, 2018.

Lonely Planet. *Lonely Planet USA's National Parks.* London: Lonely Planet, 2019.

National Geographic. *National Geographic Atlas.* Washington, DC: National Geographic, 2017.

National Geographic. *National Geographic Student World Atlas.* Washington, DC: National Geographic, 2014.

Nussbaum. "U.S. Landforms." https://mrnussbaum.com/usa/united-states-landforms.

Schnell, Lisa K. *Earth's Landforms.* Vero Beach, FL: Rourke Educational Media, 2019.

White, Mel. *National Geographic Complete National Parks of the United States.* Washington, DC: National Geographic, 2016.

World Atlas. "Landforms of Individual USA States." Updated 2019. https://www.worldatlas.com/webimage/countrys/namerica/usstates/landforms.htm.

Nonfiction—Poetry

Carpenter, Stephen, and Bruce Lanksy. *What I Did on My Summer Vacation: Kids' Favorite Funny Summer Vacation Poems.* Philadelphia, PA: Running Press, 2011.

Nesbitt, Kenn. "Transportation Poetry4Kids." Updated 2019. https://www.poetry4kids.com/poems/transportation-vacation/.

Wing, Natasha. *The Night before Summer Vacation.* St. Louis, MO: Turtleback, 2002.

My Place in the World

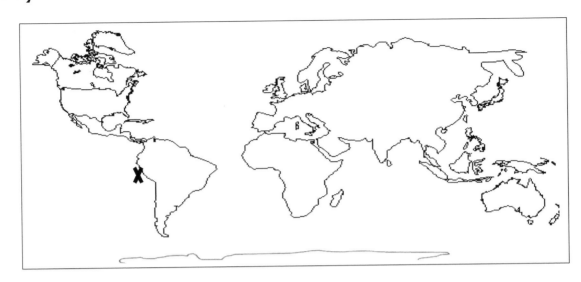

1. Following are the seven continent names. Draw a line from the continent name to their general place on the map of the world.

    (1) Africa   (2) Antarctica   (3) Asia   (4) Australia   (5) Europe

             (6) North America   (7) South America

2. Name the state where you live: _____. On the map, put an **X** close to where you live on the North American continent.

3. Compare where you live to the country of Peru in the South American continent. Do you see where the **X** is placed for Peru on the map? Is it close to where you live in North America?

What are some facts about Peru? Compare those facts to where you live. Send those facts to your friend in a message.

From: Me at Peru
To: My Friend Back Home

Peru's weather is _____ as compared to _____ where we live.

If you ever go to Peru, go swimming at the natural resource of:

Another good natural resource place to visit at Peru is:

We have two good natural resources to visit in our state too, like the following:
1.

2.

My Place in the World, Directions

Geography: Continents. My State in its continent and Peru in another continent
Grade Levels Suggested: Third Grade or Third Grade–Fifth Grades

Standards

AASL Standards

AASL Standards are listed at the start of each chapter, as each of those given standards are used in each lesson, as they are centered on students who "inquire, include, collaborate, curate, explore, and engage" (American Association of School Librarians 2017).

Common Core Language Arts Literacy Standards

CCSS.ELA-Literacy.RL.2.7 • Use the information gained from the illustrations and words in a print or digital text to demonstrate understanding of its characters, setting, or plot.

CCSS. ELA-Literacy.RL.3.1 • Ask and answer questions to demonstrate understanding of a text, referring explicitly to the text as the basis for the answers.

CCSS.ELA-Literacy.RI.3.7 • Use the information gained from illustrations (e.g., maps and photographs) and the words in a text to demonstrate understanding of the text (e.g., where, when, why, and how key events occur).

Social Studies Standards C3

D2.Geo.2.3-5. Use maps and other images to show the relationship of places and regions and their environment.

Learning Objectives

Students will

- Locate seven continents on a worksheet map.
- Compare a place in South America to their place in North America.
- Hear and discuss a fiction picture book on Peru while discussing setting and natural resources.
- Research Peru and then send a message to a person.

Suggested Teaching Team

School library and social studies teachers.

Instructional Procedure

Lessons will be a student collaborative lesson for most of the class time. Students are more often than not involved in paired or team work so that all learners have a chance to gather ideas and be involved. Assessment is ongoing observation while also checking for understanding.

1. Teachers will discuss and show that the world land mass is made up of seven continents. Teachers will then explain that students will first identify the seven continents on their worksheets and then students will compare a place in a South American continent to their place in North America.
2. Teachers will then explain and show that Peru is on the South American continent. Teacher will read and discuss the illustrations of a fiction picture book on Peru. Students will inquire, include and collaborate with others, and then explore the story's setting and natural resources as shown in that fiction picture book.

3. Students will also briefly mention two to four of the natural resources that are located in their own area of the world as well.

4. On the worksheets, student pairs will question (inquire), collaborate, gather information (curate), and explore nonfiction sources to see where the seven continents are located. Student pairs will draw lines from the continent names to the continents on the worksheet. They will also mark on the worksheet map approximately where they live in North America.

5. Student pairs will combine with another pair to make a small group. Small groups will research Peru for the weather. Then they will research some of the natural resources that would create good places to visit as a tourist (like the ocean and more).

6. On their worksheets, students will pretend to be a tourist in Peru. They will send someone a message from Peru with the researched information and so have applied their knowledge.

Recommended Resources

Fiction

Auerbach, Annie. *Meet Paddington.* New York: HarperCollins, 2014. [Paddington originated in Peru.]

Frith, Nicholas J. *Hector and Hummingbird.* New York: Scholastic, 2006.

Jo, Jong-Soon. *Festival of the Sun: Peru.* Austin, TX: Big and Small, 2016.

Nonfiction

Cane, Ella. *Continents in My World.* Minneapolis, MN: Capstone, 2014.

Cavallo, Anna. *Peru.* Minneapolis, MN: Lerner, 2012.

Cavell-Clarke, Stefi. *North America.* King's Lane, UK: BookLife, 2018.

Cavell-Clarke, Stefi. *South America.* King's Lane, UK: BookLife, 2018.

Clapper, Nikki B. *Let's Look at Peru.* Minneapolis, MN: Capstone, 2019.

Erlic, Lily. *Peru.* Alberta, CA: Weigl, 2019.

Firefly. *Firefly Atlas of North America: United States, Canada & Mexico.* Oxford, CA: Firefly, 2006.

Ganeri, Anita. *Introducing South America.* Littlemore, Oxford: Raintree, 2015.

Harris, Irene. *Earth's Continents.* New York: PowerKids Press, 2017.

Kingfisher. *The Kingfisher Student Atlas of North America.* Boston, MA: Kingfisher, 2005.

Markovics, Joyce L. *Peru.* New York: Bearport Publishing, 2017.

National Geographic. *National Geographic Kids World Atlas.* 5th ed. Washington, DC: National Geographic, 2018.

Reynolds, Toby. *Continents of the World.* New York: Crabtree, 2019.

Sherman, Jill. *Continents: What You Need to Know.* Minneapolis, MN: Capstone, 2018.

Comparing Neighbors: Canada, Mexica, and USA

Canada, Mexico, and the United States

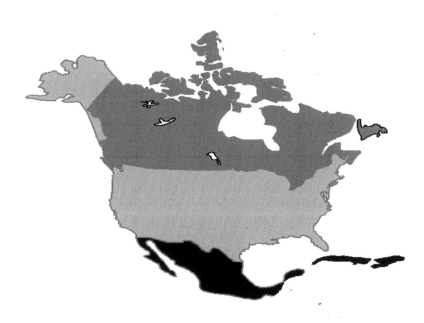

1. Draw lines from the country names to the country: **United States   Canada   Mexico**

2. The United States of America, Canada, and Mexico are in the North American continent. They are neighbors. Compare the three countries.

	Canada	Mexico	United States
Climate			
Major Mountains			
Major Rivers			
Capital			

3. Visit Canada. On your country bookmark, write the country name, and illustrate two to three places.

Comparing Neighbors: Canada, Mexico, and the United States, Directions

Geography: Climate, major landforms, capital of Canada, Mexico, and the United States
Grade Levels Suggested: Fourth Grade or Third Grade–Fifth Grades

Standards

AASL Standards

AASL Standards are listed at the start of each chapter, as each of those given standards are used in each lesson, as they are centered on students who "inquire, include, collaborate, curate, explore, and engage" (American Association of School Librarians 2017).

Common Core Language Arts Literacy Standards

CCSS.ElA-Literacy.RI.4.1 • Refer to details and examples in a text when explaining what the text says explicitly and when drawing inferences from the text.

CCSS.ELA-Literacy.RI.4.7 • Interpret the information presented visually, orally, or quantitatively (e.g., in charts, graphs, diagrams, timelines, animations, or interactive elements on web pages), and explain how the information contributes to an understanding of the text in which it appears.

Social Studies Standards C3

D2.Geo.2.3-5. Use maps and other images to show the relationship of places and regions and their environment.

Learning Objectives

Students will

- Use books and online sites to find the climate, major mountains, major rivers, and the country capital of the three neighboring countries of Canada, Mexico, and the United States.
- Draw inferences from texts.
- Interpret visual and textual sources.
- Create a bookmark about Canada and illustrate places to visit there.

Suggested Teaching Team

School library and social studies teachers.

Instructional Procedure

Lessons will be a collaborative student lesson for most of the class time. Students are more often than not involved in paired or team work so that all learners have a chance to be involved. Assessment is ongoing observation while also checking for understanding.

1. Teachers will explain that the United States has country neighbors and ask students if they know the names of the countries. Teachers will show students the countries on a map or globe. They will explain that different countries have different climates. Teachers will ask if students know places to visit in Canada and Mexico.

2. On the worksheets, students will first inquire and then explore atlases or a website in order to draw a line to that country's location from the name of the country.

3. Small student groups will compare the three neighboring countries' major mountains, major rivers, general climate, and the capitals to note on their worksheet, as they include and collaborate with each other, gather information (curate), explore, and relate to prior and present learning with nonfiction books and online sites.

4. Small groups will pretend to visit Canada and so research nonfiction books on Canada. They will need to write the name Canada on the bookmark line. On their bookmark, they will need to find and illustrate two or three places to visit in Canada.

5. Students will share their answers with the class or with small groups.

6. If there is time, students will need to find places to visit in one of the other countries.

Recommended Resources

Nonfiction

Bjorklund, Ruth. *Mexico.* New York: Cavendish, 2016.

Bowers, Vivien. *Wow Canada! Exploring This Land from Coast to Coast to Coast.* Ontario, CA: OwlsKids, 2010.

Central Intelligence Agency. "The World Factbook." Updated 2016. https://www.cia.gov/LIBRARY/publications/the-world-factbook/geos/ca.html.

Goldsworthy, Katie. *Canada.* New York: Weigl, 2015.

Gordon, Sharon. *Canada.* New York: Cavendish, 2017.

Gordon, Sharon. *United States.* New York: Cavendish, 2017.

Greil, Marlene. *United States: The Land.* New York: Crabtree, 2013.

Hurley, Michael. *United States of America.* Chicago, IL: Heinemann, 2012.

Kalman, Bobbie. *Canada: The People.* New York: Crabtree, 2010.

Kopp, Megan. *Mexico.* New York: Weigl, 2015.

Kopp, Megan. *United States.* New York: Weigl, 2015.

Murray, Julie. *Canada.* Mankato, MN: ABDO, 2014.

National Geographic. "Canada." Updated 2018. https://kids.nationalgeographic.com/explore/countries/canada/#canada-playing-hockey.jpg.

National Geographic. *Kids' Beginner's United States Atlas.* Washington, DC: National Geographic, 2016.

National Geographic. "Mexico." Updated 2018. https://kids.nationalgeographic.com/explore/countries/mexico/#mexico-dancers.jpg.

National Geographic. "United States." Updated 2018. https://kids.nationalgeographic.com/explore/countries/united-states/#united-states-golden-gate-bridge.jpg.

NationMaster. "Countries A-Z." Updated 2019. https://www.nationmaster.com/country-info/profiles.

Robinson, Joanna J. *Mexico.* Mankato, MN: Child's World, 2016.

Scholastic Grolier Online. "Land and the People Series United States." Updated 2019. http://www.factsfornow.scholastic.com/article?product_id=nbk&type=00014200ta&uid=11427556&id=1.

Scholastic Grolier Online. "Mexico: The Land." Updated 2010. http://www.scholastic.com/browse/subarticle.jsp?id=1108.

Senker, Cath. *Mexico.* Milwaukee, WI: Gareth Stevens, 2017.

Whiteford, Gary T. "Canada." Scholastic Grolier Online. Updated 2019. http://factsfornow.scholastic.com/article?product_id=nbk&type=-h0ta&uid=11437825&id=a2004360.

Williams, Colleen M. F. *Beautiful Geography. The Geography of Mexico.* Folcroft, PA: Mason Crest, 2015.

Wild about U.S. Regions

1. Draw a line from the five U.S. region names to their places on the map.

West region

Midwest region

Northeast region

Southeast region

Southwest region

2. Compare the five regions in the following chart.

Region	Major water resources to see (like an ocean, a lake, or a river)	Major land places to see (like a cave, a mountain, and more)	Other places to visit

3. Create a region list poem that simply lists each region's features.

U.S. Regions

West regions are _____.

Midwest regions are _____.

Northeast regions are _____.

Southeast regions are _____.

Southwest regions are _____.

From *New Standards-Based Lessons for the Busy Elementary School Librarian: Social Studies* by Joyce Keeling.
Santa Barbara, CA: Libraries Unlimited. Copyright © 2020.

Wild about U.S. Regions, Directions

Geography: Regions
Grade Levels Suggested: Fourth Grade or Third–Fifth Grades

Standards

AASL Standards

AASL Standards are listed at the start of each chapter, as each of those given standards are used in each lesson, as they are centered on students who "inquire, include, collaborate, curate, explore, and engage" (American Association of School Librarians 2017).

Common Core Language Arts Literacy Standards

CCSS.ELA.RL.4.2 • Determine a theme of a story, drama, or poem from details in the text; summarize the text.

CCSS.ELA-Literacy.RI.4.7 • Interpret the information presented visually, orally, or quantitatively (e.g., in charts, graphs, diagrams, timelines, animations, or interactive elements on web pages), and explain how the information contributes to an understanding of the text in which it appears.

Social Studies Standards C3

D2.Geo.2.3-5. Use maps and other images to show the relationship of places and regions and their environment.

Learning Objectives

Students will

- Locate and label the five U.S. regions on the worksheet map from visual maps.
- Hear and discuss a poem about the United States.
- Locate topics on each region, interpret that information, and create lists.
- Create a poem using a list of the U.S. regions.

Suggested Teaching Team

School library and social studies teachers.

Instructional Procedure

Lessons will be a collaborative student lesson for most of the class time. Teachers are always checking for understanding. Students are more often than not involved in paired or team work so that all learners have a chance to gather ideas and be involved. Assessment is ongoing observation while also checking for understanding.

1. This lesson concerns the five major regions of the United States. To introduce the lesson, a teacher will read a short poem about the United States and lead students in a discussion on how the poem refers to the United States.
2. Teachers will list the five regions on the board: West, Midwest, Northeast, Southwest, and Southeast.
3. Small student groups will question and collaborate with each other in order to find information about the location of the five regions on the worksheet map.

4. Small student groups will inquire, include each other, curate (gather information), and explore the five regions noting one to two major water or land resources, one to two places to visit, and other places. The classroom teachers may want to add another idea, like yearly climate.

5. Students will fill in the worksheet chart with the lists of the major researched topics.

6. Student groups will create a U.S. region's list poem on their worksheets where they will simply list the facts found. Teachers will want students to limit each region lists with four or five words. Each region will have the same number of words. Poems will be displayed with the maps in the classroom.

Recommended Resources

Nonfiction

Crabtree Publishing. *All around the US* [Book Set]. New York: Crabtree, 2012.

Purcell, Martha S. *Reading Essentials in Social Studies: Geography—U.S. Regional Road Trip* [Book Set]. Logan, IA: Perfection Learning, 2005.

Rau, Dana M. *True Books: The U.S. Regions Book Set.* Chicago, IL: Children's Press, 2012.

Robins, Maureen. *What Are the US Regions?* Vero Beach, FL: Rourke, 2012.

Smith-Liera, Danielle. *United States by Region* [Book Set]. Minneapolis, MN: Capstone, 2016.

Wiseman, Blaine. *AV2 U.S. Regions; Natural Environment* [Book Set]. Alberta, CA: Weigel, 2015.

Nonfiction Poetry

Center for Literacy in Primary Education. "List Poems." Updated 2019. https://clpe.org.uk/poetryline/poeticforms/list-poem.

Hopkins, Lee B. *Amazing Places.* New York: Lee and Low Books, 2015.

Hughes, Langston. *I, Too, Am America.* New York: Simon & Schuster, 2012.

Lewis, Patrick. *The Poetry of US: More Than 200 Poems That Celebrate the People, Places, and Passions of the United States.* Washington, DC: National Geographic, 2018.

Ringgold, Faith. *We Came to America.* New York: Knopf Books, 2016.

VanDerwater, Amy L. "List Poems. The Poem Farm." http://www.poemfarm.amylv.com/2011/04/write-list-poem.html.

With the Thirteen Colonies

Colonial Times

1. The United States started out as thirteen colonies on the east side of the United States. Look at the compass rose to see which side is **East**.

2. Find the thirteen colonies on the map. Find it on the east side of the United States of America:

Lightly color in *yellow* the New England colonies of Connecticut, Rhode Island, Massachusetts, and New Hampshire.

Lightly color in *blue* the middle colonies of New Jersey, Pennsylvania, New York, and Delaware.

Lightly color in *green* the Southern Colonies of Maryland, Virginia, North Carolina, South Carolina, and Georgia.

3. Now, be a colonist! Research and tell about the colony of _____ .

   a) Who were the people in your colony? From where did they come to the colony?

   b) What are two or more natural resources that could have been used in the colony?

With the Thirteen Colonies, Directions

Geography: Mapping, culture, and resources
Grade Levels Suggested: Fifth Grade or Third–Fifth Grades

Standards

AASL Standards

AASL Standards are listed at the start of each chapter, as each of those given standards are used in each lesson, as they are centered on students who "inquire, include, collaborate, curate, explore, and engage" (American Association of School Librarians 2017).

Common Core Language Arts Literacy Standards

CCSS.ELA-Literacy.RI.5.7 • Draw on the information from multiple print or digital sources, demonstrating the ability to locate an answer to a question quickly or to solve a problem efficiently.

CCSS.ELA-Literacy.R.I.5.9 • Integrate the information from several texts on the same topic in order to write or speak about the subject knowledgeably.

Social Studies Standards C3

D2.Geo.1.3-5. Create maps and other graphical representations of both known and unknown places.

D2.Geo.4.3-5. Describe how culture influences the way people change and adapt to their environments.

Learning Objectives

Students will

- Briefly interpret and discuss how life was in colonial times.
- Research from multiple sources, and then locate and color the thirteen colonies on the worksheet map.
- Realize the words *culture* and *natural resources*. What do they mean?
- Research and locate information on the cultures and natural resources of a selected colony.

Suggested Teaching Team

School library and social studies teachers.

Instructional Procedure

Lessons will be a collaborative student lesson for most of the class time. Students are more often than not involved in paired or team work so that all learners have a chance to gather ideas and be involved. Assessment is ongoing observation while also checking for understanding.

1. Teachers will introduce the lesson by first mentioning that the thirteen colonies were on the East Coast of America. Teachers will briefly show that location. Students will also hear a couple of examples of colonial life from a nonfiction book.
2. Teachers will explain that different groups of people came to the colonies. Those different groups can be called to have a certain type of culture, which is when a group of people together have certain behaviors or beliefs that usually pass from generation to generation.
3. Teachers will lead the group in a very brief discussion of three to four examples of natural resources that probably could be found in the colonies, like forests, rivers, and so on.

4. Student pairs or small groups will inquire, include, and collaborate with others to find the location of the thirteen colonies from an online video, an online game, or a book of various sources. Students will identify the thirteen colonies on their worksheet and lightly color those designated areas as directed.

5. Student pairs or small groups will then select a colony and become a colonist. They will explain which chosen colony they selected, the culture of the colony, and then two natural resources that they, the colonist, would have used and how they adapted to those ways. This would give students a chance to use their found evidence, connect to prior and current learning, and solve the question problems while being actively engaged.

6. If time permits, students could present their colonist research to others in the class, or individually, they could add a lifestyle of a colonist. This lesson could be expanded to the next time.

Recommended Resources

Nonfiction

Amez, Lynda. *My Life in the American Colonies*. Milwaukee, IL: Gareth Stevens, 2016.

ArtToday. "13 Colonies of America" [Interactive Game Map]. Updated 2016. http://socialstudiesforkids.com/graphics/13mapnew.htm.

Flocabulary. "The History of Colonial America." Video. Updated 2017. https://www.youtube.com/watch?v=Do4Ryapg3eU.

Hall, Brianna, Robin S. Doak, Jessica Gunderson, and Steven Otfinoski. *Smithsonian—Exploring the 13 Colonies* [Book Set]. Minneapolis, MN: Capstone, 2017.

Jacobson, Bray. *The Thirteen Colonies*. New York: Gareth Stevens, 2018.

Lineville, Rich. *The 13 American Colonies to Learn Their Names and Shapes with Jokes and Facts*. Scotts Valley, CA: CreateSpace Independent Publishing, 2018.

Nussbaum. "Mr. N 365 13 Colonies Interactive" [Interactive Map]. https://www.mrnussbaum.com/13int.

Omoth, Tyler. *Establishing the American Colonies*. Mendota Heights, MN: North Star, 2018.

PowerKids Press. *Spotlight on the 13th Colonies* [Book Set]. New York: Power Kids, 2017.

Rajczak, Kristen. *Life in the American Colonies* [Book Set]. Milwaukee, WI: Gareth Stevens, 2014.

Raum, Elizabeth. *The Scoop on Clothes, Homes, and Daily Life in Colonial America*. Minneapolis, MN: Capstone, 2017.

Savage, Julie A. *Colonial Times Picture Book*. San Francisco, CA: Green Apple Lessons Inc., 2017.

Zoeller. "Mr. Zoller's Thirteen Colonies Series." Video. Updated 2011. https://www.youtube.com/watch?v=4ScZh2-QLOE&list=PL9bDHRx3YbkV_rZLEF-eg8I6v080oCnS4.

U.S. Coordinates

The United States of America States and the Thirteen Colonies

1. Label each state with the two-letter state abbreviations. For instance, AL stands for Alabama.

2. On the map, lightly circle the approximate location of the thirteen colonies in the eastern United States.

3. Play the coordinates game! Compare the location of the states and then the thirteen colonies. Use coordinates. Coordinates are the latitude and longitude or numbers around the map.

> (1) First answer the following questions. (2) Now play the game! To another, give one of your coordinates set, say if it is a state or colony, and then see who can give the name of the state or colony the fastest.

Write the coordinate (latitude and longitude) numbers for states:

State_____   Coordinates _____ , _____

State _____   Coordinates _____ , _____

Write coordinates for a colony.

Colony_____   Coordinates ___ , ___

U.S. Coordinates, Directions

Geography: Latitude and longitude coordinates
Grade Levels Suggested: Fifth Grade or Third–Fifth Grades

Standards

AASL Standards

AASL Standards are listed at the start of each chapter, as each of those given standards are used in each lesson, as they are centered on students who "inquire, include, collaborate, curate, explore, and engage" (American Association of School Librarians 2017).

Common Core Language Arts Literacy Standards

CCSS.ELA-Literacy.RI.5.7 • Draw on the information from multiple print or digital sources, demonstrating the ability to locate an answer to a question quickly or to solve a problem efficiently.

CCSS.ELA-Literacy.R.I.5.9 • Integrate the information from several texts on the same topic in order to write or speak about the subject knowledgeably.

Social Studies Standards C3

D2.Geo.2.3-5. Use maps and other images to show the relationship of places and regions and their environment.

Learning Objectives

Students will

- Locate and label the two-letter abbreviations for the U.S. states on the worksheet map.
- Locate and label the thirteen colonies.
- Use map coordinates on their worksheets and in a game.

Suggested Teaching Team

School library and social studies teachers.

Instructional Procedure

Lessons will be a collaborative student lesson for most of the class time. Students are more often than not involved in paired or team work so that all learners have a chance to gather ideas and be involved. Assessment is ongoing observation while also checking for understanding.

1. This lesson will most likely take another lesson time to complete.
2. Teachers will show and discuss the definitions of coordinates and longitude and latitude with a video or book resource.
3. Teachers will quickly show and discuss the very general location of the thirteen colonies on a map, like noting the eastern part of the country. Small student groups will research and locate the location of the thirteen colonies on the worksheet map.
4. Students will switch thinking to look at the location of all fifty states. Student groups will question, collaborate, and find information for the two-letter abbreviations for U.S. states, as well as each state's location on a map. Students will use the two-letter state abbreviations on the worksheet map to identify the location of each state.

5. Student groups will quickly compare as they use prior and current knowledge to strategically solve the location of the U.S. states as compared to the location of the thirteen colonies while playing a game.

6. Student groups will break into pairs. Student pairs will question, collaborate, and write the coordinates of two states and then for colony on their worksheet.

7. Student groups will take turns trying to answer the coordinates game as given by student pairs. Teachers will designate a time limit.

Recommended Resources

Nonfiction

Britannica Kids. "13 American Colonies." Updated 2019. https://kids.britannica.com/students/assembly/view/192317.

Infoplease. "State Abbreviations and State Postal Codes." Updated 2018. https://www.infoplease.com/state-abbreviations-and-state-postal-codes.

Marsh, Carole. *The 13 Colonies: A New Life in a New World!* Atlanta, GA: Gallopade, 2010.

McNally, Rand. *2019 Rand McNally Large Scale Road Atlas.* Chicago, IL: Rand McNally Press, 2018.

National Geographic. *National Geographic Kids United States Atlas.* Washington, DC: National Geographic, 2017.

National Geographic. *National Geographic Student World Atlas.* 5th ed. Washington, DC: National Geographic, 2019.

OnTheWorldMap. "USA State Abbreviations Map." Updated 2019. http://ontheworldmap.com/usa/usa-state-abbreviations-map.html.

Oxford University Press. *Atlas of the World.* 25th ed. New York: Oxford University Press, 2018.

Quinlan, Julia. *Latitude, Longitude, and Direction.* New York: PowerKids Press, 2012.

Rajczak, Kristen. *Latitude and Longitude.* New York: Gareth Stevens, 2015.

Roble Education. "Dr. Nagler's Laboratory: Longitude and Latitude." Video. Updated 2015. https://www.youtube.com/watch?v=cTrsvGytGG0.

Roble Education. "Dr. Nagler's Laboratory: Plotting Coordinates." Updated 2015. https://www.youtube.com/watch?v=h26o9GKusK4.

Stoltman, Joan. *20 Fun Facts about the 13 Colonies.* New York: Gareth Stevens, 2015.

Teacher Created Materials, and Sharon Coan. *Looking at Maps.* Huntington Beach, CA: Teacher Created Materials, 2008.

White, James. "Longitude and Latitude." Video. 2010. https://www.youtube.com/watch?v=-0c1idtn3e8.

World Atlas. "Original Thirteen Colonies." Updated 2018. https://www.worldatlas.com/webimage/countrys/namerica/usstates/colonies.htm.

World Atlas. "US States Abbreviation Map." Updated 2018. https://www.worldatlas.com/webimage/countrys/usaabrv.htm.

Chapter 4

School Librarian and Social Studies Teachers and History

This chapter focuses on topics of history from the Social Studies Standards, along with the information library literacy standards and language arts standards. The teacher librarians partner with the elementary social studies teachers to provide excellence in instruction with engaging lessons, with library resources and online resources, as students collaborate with others in order to create learning. Lessons are approximately twenty minutes long and packed with resources and based on learning standards.

If not using some of these specific standards, the educator will apply other standards. Likewise, the educator can pick and choose any of the three sets of standards—the library standards for learners, Social Studies Standards, and language arts/literacy standards—or use all of those standards as applied in each lesson. The mixture of social studies, language arts/literacy, and library or information literacy skills and resources provides well-rounded opportunities for successful learning.

This chapter begins with lessons for kindergarten, with those lessons being usable for other lower elementary grades, and then the lessons move upward to the fifth grade. Grade levels are not narrowly assigned per lesson but are suggested. Furthermore, this book not only engages all learners but also offers lessons that can be intermingled for other elementary grades. There are many resources that have been tested before being suggested with each lesson, offering more teaching opportunities. However, the main focus is student-engaged learning—educators teaching through helpful plans and resources, all based on standards.

Standards

AASL Standards

AASL Standards Framework for Learners

AASL Standards for Learners are listed at the start of each chapter, as each of those given standards are used in each lesson, as they are centered on students who "inquire, include, collaborate, curate, explore, and engage."

American Association of School Librarians. "AASL Standards Framework for Learners." Updated 2017. https://standards.aasl.org/framework.

AASL Standards Framework for Learners encourage learners to

1. Inquire through such means as questioning, using evidence, connecting to prior knowledge, making decisions, and more.
2. Include through such means as discussing, examining other's views, reflecting, and more.
3. Collaborate through participating, obtaining feedback, solving problems with others to connect shared learning, and more.
4. Curate through such means as determining a need and then gathering and organizing information from a variety of accurate resources, reflecting, and more.
5. Explore through such means as reading, writing, creating, asking questions, solving problems, expressing being curious, reflecting, and more.
6. Engage through such means as applying and evaluating information and sources to learning in an ethical way, including avoiding plagiarism and more.

Excerpted and adapted from *National School Library Standards for Learners, School Librarians, and School Libraries* by the American Association of School Librarians, a division of the American Library Association, copyright © 2018 American Library Association. Available for download at https://standards.aasl.org/framework. Used with permission.

Social Studies Standards—the Inquiry Arc of the C3 (College, Career, and Civic Life) Framework

History K-2
D2.His.2.K-2. Compare life in the past to the present.
D2.His.3.K-2. Create questions on individuals and groups who made an important historical change.
D2.His.16.K-2. Select the reasons that explain a historical event or development.

History 3-5
D2.His.2.3-5. Compare life in certain historical times to life today.
D2.His.3.3-5. Create questions on individuals and groups who made historical changes.
D2.His.16.3-5.Use evidence to create a claim about the past.

National Council for the Social Studies. *Social Studies for the Next Generation: Purposes, Practices, and Implications of the College, Career, and Civic Life (C3) Framework for Social Studies State Standards.* Silver Spring, MD. 2013.

Common Core Standards—Literacy

Common Course Language Arts Literacy Standards or CCSS, which are given in the introductory standards section of the book, are seen with each lesson. These standards are too lengthy to be given here at the start of each chapter, but they are seen as needed for each lesson. For a complete look at this book's Common Core Standards in Literacy, refer to the introduction section.

Educators may prefer to intermingle other or additional standards or simply select some or all of the given standards. Each lesson holds a wealth of resources for educators to pick and choose from to support the standards-based learning and subsequently lessons. The standards are the foundation or framework of learning, but the teachers hold the key.

Tepees

Some early American Indians lived in tepees. Where do you live? Draw it in the box below.

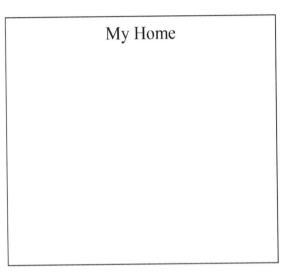

My Home

How would you live if you lived in a tepee? Draw pictures below.

Tepees, Directions

History: Comparing homes from some early American tepees
Grade Levels Suggested: Kindergarten or Kindergarten–Second Grades

Standards

AASL Standards

AASL Standards are listed at the start of each chapter, as each of those given standards are used in each lesson, as they are centered on students who "inquire, include, collaborate, curate, explore, and engage" (American Association of School Librarians 2017).

Common Core Language Arts Literacy Standards

CCSS.ELA-Literacy.RI.K.2 • With prompting and support, identify the main topic and retell key details of a text.

CCSS.ELA-Literacy.RL.K.1 • With prompting and support, ask and answer questions about key details in a text.

Social Studies Standards C3

D2.His.2.K-2. Compare life in the past to the present.

Learning Objectives

Students will

- Compare a teepee to their home through class discussions and research.
- Hear and see a picture fiction book and discuss setting and major events.
- Illustrate their home next to the teepee.
- Research and find key details on how American Indians lived many years ago that is different from how the students live now, and illustrate those facts.

Suggested Teaching Team

School library and social studies teachers.

Instructional Procedure

Lessons will be a collaborative student lesson for most of the class time. Students are more often than not involved in paired or team work so that all learners have a chance to gather ideas and be involved. Assessment is ongoing observation while also checking for understanding.

1. Teachers will introduce the lesson by showing and reading parts of a fiction picture book about an early American Indian/Native American life. Teachers will ask students what they learned about how an early American Indian lived, as seen from the book setting and major events.
2. Teachers will explain that years ago, American Indians, like the Plains Indians, lived in a certain place (the Plains) and in a teepee (tipi). Students will see a teepee picture.
3. On worksheets, students will draw their home as compared to the teepee home.
4. Teachers will explain that small student groups will use a nonfiction book to question, explore, and solve the problem on finding more information on how early American Indians lived.
5. Small student groups will then inquire, collaborate with others in the group, and find detailed information and two facts from nonfiction books about how early American Indians lived.

6. Individuals will become engaged as they illustrate their found facts next to the bottom teepee.

7. Students will color their sheets. If time permits, they will share their work with the class.

Recommended Resources

Fiction

Bruchac, Joseph, and Robert F. Goetzl. *Many Nations: An Alphabet of Native America*. New York: Scholastic, 2004.

Shoulders, Michael, and Debbie Shoulders. *D Is for Drum.* Mankato, MN: Sleeping Bear Press, 2006.

Thomas, Penny M. *Powwow Counting in Cree*. Custer, WA: Highwater Press, 2013.

Nonfiction

Dinmont, Kerry. *Homes Past and Present.* Minneapolis, MN: Lerner, 2019.

Higgins, Nadia. *Homes Then and Now.* Minneapolis, MN: Jump!, 2019.

Knight, P. V. *Native American Homes: From Longhouses to Wigwams.* Milwaukee, WI: Gareth Stevens, 2018.

Manning, Jack. *Tepees.* Minneapolis, MN: Capstone, 2014.

Matzke, Ann. *My Life as a Native American.* Vero Beach, FL: Rourke, 2013.

McGovern, Ann. *If You Lived with the Sioux Indians.* New York: Scholastic, 2014.

Trumbauer, Lisa. *The First Americans.* Chicago, IL: Heinemann, 2016.

Toys

What were some toys from a long time ago?

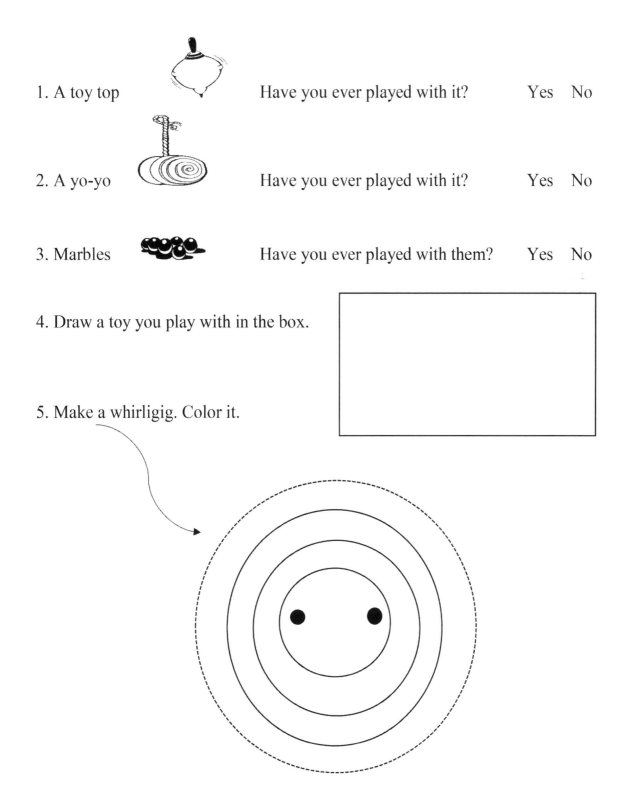

1. A toy top   Have you ever played with it?   Yes   No

2. A yo-yo   Have you ever played with it?   Yes   No

3. Marbles   Have you ever played with them?   Yes   No

4. Draw a toy you play with in the box.

5. Make a whirligig. Color it.

Toys, Directions

History: Comparing games and toys from colonial times to today
Grade Levels Suggested: Kindergarten or Kindergarten–Second Grades

Standards

AASL Standards

AASL Standards are listed at the start of each chapter, as each of those given standards are used in each lesson, as they are centered on students who "inquire, include, collaborate, curate, explore, and engage" (American Association of School Librarians 2017).

Common Core Language Arts Literacy Standards

CCSS.ELA-Literacy.RL.K.1 • With prompting and support, ask and answer questions about key details in a text.
CCSS.ELA-Literacy.RI.K.2 • With prompting and support, identify the main topic and retell key details of a text.

Social Studies Standards C3

D2.His.2.K-2. Compare life in the past to the present.

Learning Objectives

Students will

- Compare toys and games from colonial times to now.
- Briefly hear and discuss colonial times.
- Research nonfiction sources finding key details for games and toys.
- Complete their worksheets and make a colonial toy.

Suggested Teaching Team

School library and social studies teachers.

Instructional Procedure

Lessons will be a collaborative student lesson for most of the class time. Students are more often than not involved in paired or team work so that all learners have a chance to gather ideas and be involved. Assessment is ongoing observation while also checking for understanding.

1. Worksheets will need to be run off on card stock. Students will each need a three-foot string or yarn to make the whirligig toy.
2. Teachers will first identify a pilgrim or colonial person. Teachers will skim and show a small portion of a colonial-time nonfiction book and its illustrations. Teachers will ask students to question, collaborate with the class, and reflect how the lives in pilgrim (colonial) times were different then how the students live now.
3. Teachers will show one or two illustrations from a book on games in the past and briefly discuss how to play those games.
4. From nonfiction books, student groups will question (inquire), include and collaborate within the group, gather and reflect the information, and find three to five toys and perhaps a game from the past. Engaged student groups will share and discuss the illustrations with the rest of the class.

5. Teachers will guide students with their worksheet work. Students will color their worksheet including the bottom whirligig shape.

6. If students are making an actual whirligig, students will cut out the card stock worksheet whirligig in one big circular shape. Students will lightly color the blank side. Teachers will help students punch a hole in the two black holes on the whirligig. Teachers will help students string a three-foot string or yarn through the holes and tie the string ends together. To make it work, students will lightly twist the string with the whirligig shape in the middle and then put their fingers in the string loops and pull to untwist.

Recommended Resources

Nonfiction—Colonial Times

Arnaz, Lynda. *My Life in the American Colonies*. Milwaukee, WI: Gareth Stevens, 2016.

Goodman, Sharon. *Pilgrims of Plymouth*. Washington, DC: National Geographic, 2001.

Mara, Wil. *If You Were a Kid in the Thirteen Colonies*. New York: Children's Press, Scholastic, 2017.

Waters, Kate. *Sarah Morton's Day: A Day in the Life of a Pilgrim Girl*. New York: Scholastic, 2008.

Nonfiction—Toys/Games

Boothroyd, Jennifer. *From Marbles to Video Games*. Minneapolis, MN: Lerner, 2011.

Dinmont, Kerry. *Toys and Games Past and Present*. Minneapolis, MN: Lerner, 2019.

Higgins, Nadia. *Toys Then and Now*. Orlando, FL: Pogo, 2019.

Kalman, Bobbie. *Toys and Games Then and Now*. New York: Crabtree, 2014.

Nelson, Robin. *Toys and Games Then and Now*. Minneapolis, MN: Lerner, 2003.

Rutter, James, eHow Contributor. "What Games Did Children Play in Colonial Times?" Updated 2014. https://acegames4usdotorg.wordpress.com/2014/07/18/what-games-did-children-play-in-colonial-times/.

Thomas, Mark. *Fun and Games in Colonial America*. New York: Rosen, 2002.

Whirligigs

Buckwald, Barbara. "Colonial Children's Games." Updated 2002. http://www.pencaderheritage.org/main/teachtool/games.

Monclare Museum. "Whirligig. Toy." https://www.mountclare.org/education/MakeYourOwnWhirligigToy.

School Time

How were schools in the past different from schools now?

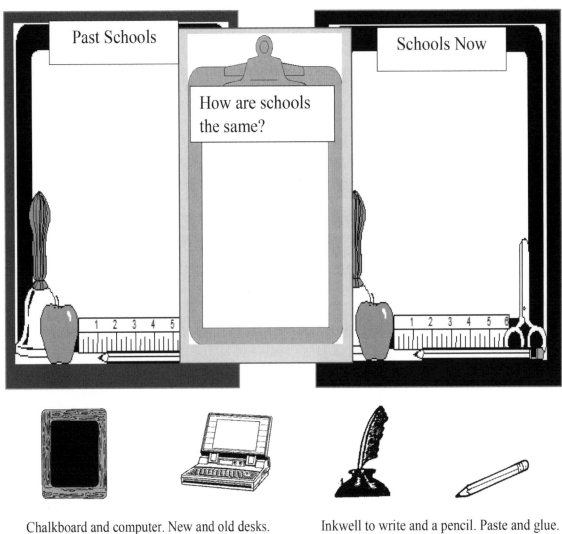

Past Schools

How are schools the same?

Schools Now

Chalkboard and computer. New and old desks.

Inkwell to write and a pencil. Paste and glue.

School Time, Directions

History: History comparison of schools now and then
Grade Levels Suggested: First Grade or Kindergarten–Second Grades

Standards

AASL Standards

AASL Standards are listed at the start of each chapter, as each of those given standards are used in each lesson, as they are centered on students who "inquire, include, collaborate, curate, explore, and engage" (American Association of School Librarians 2017).

Common Core Language Arts Literacy Standards

CCSS.ELA-Literacy.RL.1.1 • Ask and answer questions about key details in a text.
CCSS.ELA-Literacy.RL.1.7 • Use illustrations and details in a story to describe its characters, settings, or events.

Social Studies Standards C3

D2.His.2.K-2. Compare life in the past to the present.
D2.His.16.K-2. Select the reasons that explain a historical event or development.

Learning Objectives

Students will

- Discuss the events or main plot of an easy fiction book after hearing the story.
- Discuss and compare past and present schools to their school after hearing and seeing a nonfiction book about past and present schools with details pointed out.
- Research past and present schools.
- Complete their worksheets to illustrate the differences and similarities of past and present schools.
- Hear a school poem.

Suggested Teaching Team

School library and social studies teachers.

Instructional Procedure

Lessons will be a collaborative student lesson for most of the class time. Teachers are always checking for understanding. Students are more often than not involved in paired or team work so that all learners have a chance to gather ideas and be involved. Assessment is ongoing observation while also checking for understanding.

1. Settings and then plot or main events will be discussed after teachers read a humorous fiction picture book about school.
2. Teachers will show and discuss a nonfiction book that shows schools in the past and present. Teachers will ask students if there were some things in their current classroom that were the same and then different from the book illustrations with a past school.
3. Student groups will question, include and collaborate within the group, gather information, explore, and engage by researching and comparing past to present schools from nonfiction books. Students will also relate information to prior and present information, as they locate four differences between present and past schools.

4. Teachers will discuss the worksheet directions. Students will answer their worksheet either by illustrating or by writing from their research. If desired, students could also draw a line from the bottom pictures to the past or present. Teachers will need to describe what each bottom item is; for example, the inkwell was used like a pen is used today. Teachers will also question the reasons for the changes for schools.

5. Students will share their results. Teachers will ask students to again compare results with others and with their present classroom.

6. Teachers will finally read and discuss the main plot of some humorous school poems.

Recommended Resources

Fiction

Bowen, Anne. *I Know an Old Teacher.* Minneapolis, MN: Carolrhoda, 2008.

Calmenson, Stephanie. *Our Principal Is a Wolf.* New York: Aladdin Quix, 2018.

Cox, Judy. *Don't Be Silly, Mrs. Mille!* New York: Marshall Cavendish, 2010.

Griswell, Kim T. *Rufus Goes to School.* New York: Sterling Children's Books, 2013.

Grogan, John. *Marley Goes to School.* New York: Harper, 2012.

Parish, Herman. *Amelia Bedelia's First Day of School.* New York: HarperCollins, 2015.

Tuma, Refe, and Susan Tuma. *What the Dinosaurs Did at School.* New York: Little, Brown Books, 2017.

Wohnoutka, Mike. *Dad's First Day.* New York: Bloomsbury, 2015.

Nonfiction

Baraasch, Lynne. *A Country Schoolhouse.* New York: Farrar, Straus and Giroux, 2004.

Boothroyd, Jennifer. *From Chalkboards to Computers: How Schools Have Changed.* Minneapolis, MN: Lerner, 2011.

Dinmont, Kerry. *Schools Past and Present.* Minneapolis, MN: Lerner, 2018.

Kay, Verla, and S. D. Schindler. *Hornbooks and Inkwells.* New York: G.P. Putnam's Sons, 2011.

Lee, Sally. *School Long Ago and Today.* Minneapolis, MN: Capstone, 2015.

Nelson, Robin. *School Then and Now.* Minneapolis, MN: Lerner, 2003.

Rissman, Rebecca. *Going Back to School: Comparing Past and Present.* Chicago, IL: Heinemann, 2014.

Nonfiction—Poetry

Greenburg, David. *Super Silly School Poems.* London, UK: Orchard Books, 2014.

Horton, Joan. *I Brought My Rat for Show-and-Tell: And Other Funny School Poems.* New York: Penguin, 2013.

Lansky, Bruce. *My Teacher's in Detention: Kids' Favorite Funny School Poems.* Riverton, WY: Meadowbrook Press, 2006.

Nesbitt, Kenn. *When the Teacher Isn't Looking: And Other Funny School Poems.* Riverton, WY: Meadowbrook Press, 2005.

Prelutsky, Jack. *What a Day It Was at School!* New York: Greenwillow, 2009.

Schmidt, Amy. *Back to Dog-Gone School.* New York: Random House, 2016.

Around the World in America

 Different families have differing traditions, and families in America come from all over. Traditions develop over many years, from food, clothing, music, or dance and special family times.

1. Listen to a book about a family tradition. Where could the traditional food have come from?

Mexico   China   or _____

2. Draw the tradition.

3. Make a booklet about your family's traditions.

My Family's Traditions

My Name:

My family's tradition is:

Around the World in America, Directions

History: Cultures
Grade Levels Suggested: First Grade or First–Second Grades

Standards

AASL Standards

AASL Standards are listed at the start of each chapter, as each of those given standards are used in each lesson, as they are centered on students who "inquire, include, collaborate, curate, explore, and engage" (American Association of School Librarians 2017).

Common Core Language Arts Literacy Standards

CCSS.ELA-Literacy.RL.1.1 • Ask and answer questions about key details in a text.
CCSS.ELA-Literacy.RL.1.3 • Describe characters, settings, and major events in a story, using key details.
CCSS.ELA-Literacy.RL.1.5 • Explain major differences between books that tell stories and books that give information, drawing on a wide reading of a range of text types.

Social Studies Standards C3

D2.His.2.K-2. Compare life in the past to the present.

Learning Objectives

Students will

- Discuss and understand a family tradition.
- Hear, see, and discuss key details of either a video or a nonfiction book on tradition.
- Hear, see, and discuss main plot and setting of a family tradition fiction picture book.
- Answer worksheet questions, including making their own tradition booklet.

Suggested Teaching Team

School library and social studies teachers.

Instructional Procedure

Lessons will be a collaborative student lesson for most of the class time. Teachers are always checking for understanding. Students are more often than not involved in paired or team work so that all learners have a chance to gather ideas and be involved. Assessment is ongoing observation while also checking for understanding.

1. Teachers will first select a culture or family traditions from China, Mexico, or Native Americans and read a fictional picture book about that topic.
2. Teachers will define family traditions. Students will question family tradition definitions. The worksheets have some family tradition definitions. Teachers will show traditions either in a video or as seen in a nonfiction book, which will then be discussed. Teachers will ask whether students know if their family came from a different country and one thing that their family did in that country. Teachers will tell students that some family traditions do not change from past history.
3. Teachers will read and discuss the chosen picture fiction book from China, Mexico, or Native American cultures. Students will be led in a discussion on main plot or events concerning the cultural tradition as seen in the book. Students will relate traditions to some students' family traditions.

4. Student pairs will inquire, collaborate, and explore worksheets questions on the discussed fictional picture book.

5. Individual students will question and then create a booklet about their family traditions. There are two booklet shapes on the bottom of the worksheet. Students will draw their family or perhaps themselves in the square of the booklet cover. They will also write their name. On the next page, they will draw their family tradition (some may have to guess). Students will cut out the two pages of their booklet.

6. If time permits, students will create additional two or three blank pages for their booklet, as they trace the size of those pages from their booklet's first two pages. Then, they can add more family tradition pages. Also, they could have a family member create a page.

Recommended Resources

Nonfiction—General Traditions

Aloian, Molly. *Cultural Traditions in the United States*. New York: Crabtree, 2014.
Cultural Traditions in My World [Book Set]. New York: Crabtree, 2013–2018.
DK. *Readers: Holiday! Celebrations around the World*. New York: DK, 2013.
Duffield, Katy. *Celebrations around the World*. St. Louis, MO: Ready Readers, 2018.
Higgins, Melissa. *We All Come from Different Cultures*. Minneapolis, MN: Capstone, 2012.
Murphy, Charles. *Food around the World*. Milwaukee, WI: Gareth Stevens, 2017.
Paul, Miranda. "The World's Family." Video. Updated 2015. https://www.youtube.com/watch?v=ni_at59TzMA&index=1 &list=PL7QZnhsBRsJTOSOAFTYhDu3TsMmpgIkDh.
Pettiford, Rebecca. *Different Cultures*. North Mankato, MN: Bullfrog Books, 2018.
Robbins, Maureen. *One Land, Many Cultures*. Vero Beach, FL: Rourke, 2012.

Fiction—Chinese Traditions

Lendroth, Susan. *Natsumi!* New York: G.P. Putnam's Sons, 2018.
Lin, Grace. *Dim Sum for Everyone*. Edmond, OK: Dragonfly, 2013.
Lin, Grace. *Fortune Cookies Fortunes*. Edmond, OK: Dragonfly Books, 2006.
Lo-Hagan, Virginia. *PoPo's Lucky Chinese New Year*. Mankato, MN: Sleeping Bear Press, 2017.
Uegaki, Chieri. *Suki's Kimono*. Toronto, ON: Kids Can Press, 2005.
Wei, Jie. *Home for Chinese New Year: A Story Told in English and Chinese*. Shanghai, China: Better Link Press, 2017.
Yu, Li-Qiong. *A New Year's Reunion*. Somerville, MA: Candlewick, 2013.

Nonfiction—Chinese Traditions

Schuh, Mari. *Crayola: Chinese New Year Colors*. New York: Lerner, 2018.
Stuart, Carrie. *Chinese*. New York: Rosen, 2007.

Fiction—Latino/Mexican Traditions

McCormack, Caren M. *The Fiesta Dress: A Quinceanera Tale*. New York: Marshall Cavendish, 2012.
Thong, Roseanne. *Green Is a Chile Pepper: A Book of Colors*. San Francisco, CA: Chronicle, 2016.
Witte, Anna. *Lola's Fandango*. Cambridge, MA: Barefoot Books, 2018.
Zepeda, Gwendolyn. *Growing Up with Tamales = Los Tamales De Ana*. Arvada, CO: Lorito Books, 2009.

Nonfiction—Latino/Mexican Traditions

Gonzalez Perez, Dr. Ma. Alma. *Traditions Alphabet Book* [Bilingual English/Spanish]. Zapata TX: Del-Alma Publications, 2019.

Nelson, Robin. *Crayola: Cinco De Mayo Colors*. Minneapolis, MN: Lerner, 2018.

Peppas, Lynn. *Cultural Traditions in Mexico*. New York: Crabtree, 2012.

Thong, Roseanne G. *One Is a Pinata: A Book of Numbers*. San Francisco, CA: Chronicle Books, 2019.

Thong, Roseanne. *Round Is a Tortilla*. San Francisco, CA: Chronicle, 2015.

Fiction—Native American Traditions

Boyden, Linda. *Powwow's Coming*. Albuquerque, NM: University of New Mexico Press, 2007.

Francis, DeCora Lee. *Kunu's Basket: A Story from Indian Island*. Thomaston, ME: Tilbury House, 2015.

Minnema, Cheryl Kay. *Hungry Johnny*. St. Paul, MN: Minnesota Historical Society, 2014.

Smith, Cynthia Leitch. *Jingle Dancer*. New York: HarperCollins, 2000.

Sorell, Taci. *We Are Grateful: Otsaliheliga*. Watertown, MA: Charlesbridge, 2018.

Nonfiction—Native American Traditions

Mikoley, Kate. *Native American Ceremonies and Celebrations: From Potlatches to Powwows*. Milwaukee, WI: Gareth Stevens, 2018.

Thomas, Penny M. *Powwow Counting in Cree*. Custer, WA: Highwater Press, 2013.

Covered Wagon

1. Draw yourself driving the wagon. On the white, covered part of the wagon, draw something that would have happened on the wagon trail.

2. How has travel on land changed from the covered wagon times?

3. On the following black line, make a timeline of how travel on land has changed.

Travel on Land Timeline

Cut out the following ways to travel. Put them on the timeline from oldest to new.

From *New Standards-Based Lessons for the Busy Elementary School Librarian: Social Studies* by Joyce Keeling.
Santa Barbara, CA: Libraries Unlimited. Copyright © 2020.

Covered Wagon, Directions

History: Concise history of land travel
Grade Levels Suggested: Second Grade or Second–First Grades

Standards

AASL Standards

AASL Standards are listed at the start of each chapter, as each of those given standards are used in each lesson, as they are centered on students who "inquire, include, collaborate, curate, explore, and engage" (American Association of School Librarians 2017).

Common Core Language Arts Literacy Standards

CCSS.ELA-Literacy.RL.2.7 • Use the information gained from the illustrations and words in a print or digital text to demonstrate understanding of its characters, setting, or plot.
CCSS.ELA-Literacy.RI.2.1 • Ask and answer such questions as who, what, where, when, why, and how to demonstrate understanding of the key details in a text.

Social Studies Standards C3

D2.His.2.K-2. Compare life in the past to the present.
D2.His.16.K-2. Select the reasons that explain a historical event or development.

Learning Objectives

Students will

- Discuss the events and settings of a picture fiction book after hearing the story.
- Use key details to research the history of land transportation with emphasis on road travel.
- Complete their worksheets, which includes a timeline.

Suggested Teaching Team

School library and social studies teachers.

Instructional Procedure

Lessons will be a collaborative student lesson for most of the class time. Students are more often than not involved in paired or team work so that all learners have a chance to gather ideas and be involved. Assessment is ongoing observation while also checking for understanding.

1. Settings, events, and the main plot will be discussed after teachers read an easy reading fiction book about a covered wagon. Teachers will explain that covered wagons were a way to get across the land in the past.
2. Teachers will explain the concept word *transportation*. Students will be told that they will study the history of moving things from place to place using wheels.
3. Small student groups will question, explore, and engage with the detailed facts in nonfiction books on the history of transportation. They will share what they have found about the history of things on wheels that traveled on roads or trails.
4. Teachers will explain and show that in pioneer days, the pioneers used wagon wheel travel. Next came older-type bicycles, early cars, and then cars today.

5. On worksheets, students will draw themselves driving a covered wagon. Then they will draw an event from the teacher-read fiction book.

6. Teachers will guide the class as they consider how driving on roads or trails has changed from covered wagons to current road travel and why it has changed.

7. Students will cut a circle around the vehicles from the bottom of the worksheet and then glue those in order on the black line according to the oldest to the newest. Students will be making a pictorial timeline.

Recommended Resources

Fiction

Applegate, Katherine. *The Buffalo Storm*. New York: Houghton Mifflin Harcourt, 2014.

Dundy, Melanie R. *The Oregon Trail: Ollie's Great Adventure*. MDCT Publishing, 2018. (Just read part of this one.)

Hancher, Adam. *The Little Pioneer*. New York: Doubleday, 2018.

Hopkinson, Deborah. *Apples to Oregon: Being the (Slightly) True Narrative of How a Brave Pioneer Father Brought Apples, Peaches, Pears, Plums, Grapes, and Cherries (and Children) across the Plains*. New York: Aladdin, 2008.

Levine, Ellen, and Elroy Freem. *If You Traveled West in a Covered Wagon*. New York: Scholastic, 2016.

Murphy, Patricia. *DK Readers L2: Journey of a Pioneer*. New York: DK, 2008.

Nonfiction—Colonial Times

Dinmont, Kerry. *Transportation Past and Present*. Minneapolis, MN: Lerner, 2019.

Higgins, Nadia. *Transportation Then and Now*. Orlando, FL: Pogo, 2019.

Matzke, Ann. *My Life as a Pioneer*. Vero Beach, FL: Rourke, 2012.

Morley, Jacqueline. *You Wouldn't Want to Be an American Pioneer: A Wilderness You'd Rather Not Tame*. London, UK: Franklin Watts, 2012.

Simons, Lisa M. B. *Transportation: Long Ago and Today*. Minneapolis, MN: Capstone, 2015.

Spengler, Kremema. *An Illustrated Timeline of Transportation*. Mankato, MN: Picture Window Books, 2012.

Thomas, Ron, and Shirley Sydenham. "Road Transportation: A Timeline." Updated 2018. http://www.kidcyber.com.au/road-transport-a-timeline.

What's Next Benjamin Franklin?

1. Who was Benjamin Franklin? _____

_____

_____

2. What happened when Benjamin Franklin used the kite? _____

_____

3. Draw two other things that Benjamin Franklin created. Draw them in Benjamin Franklin's hands.

4. What is something that Benjamin Franklin did that has helped your neighborhood?

_____

_____

What's Next Benjamin Franklin? Directions

History: History of Benjamin Franklin and his inventions that helped
Grade Levels Suggested: First Grade or Kindergarten–Second Grades

Standards

AASL Standards

AASL Standards are listed at the start of each chapter, as each of those given standards are used in each lesson, as they are centered on students who "inquire, include, collaborate, curate, explore, and engage" (American Association of School Librarians 2017).

Common Core Language Arts Literacy Standards

CCSS.ELA-Literacy.RL.2.7 • Use the information gained from the illustrations and words in a print or digital text to demonstrate understanding of its characters, setting, or plot.

CCSS.ELA-Literacy.RI.2.1 • Ask and answer such questions as who, what, where, when, why, and how to demonstrate understanding of the key details in a text.

Social Studies Standards C3

D2.His.3.K-2. Create questions on individuals and groups who made an important historical change.

Learning Objectives

Students will

- Discuss the setting, character, and the main plot of a picture fiction book after hearing the story and seeing the illustrations.
- Hear and discuss key details of a nonfiction book or video on Benjamin Franklin.
- Research more about Benjamin Franklin.
- Answer the questions given in their worksheets.

Suggested Teaching Team

School library and social studies teachers.

Instructional Procedure

Lessons will be a collaborative student lesson for most of the class time. Teachers are always checking for understanding. Students are more often than not involved in paired or team work so that all learners have a chance to gather ideas and be involved. Assessment is ongoing observation while also checking for understanding.

1. Settings, character, and the main plot will be discussed after teachers read a humorous fiction picture book about an inventor's character or read and discuss the book by Rosentock about Benjamin Franklin creating a library. Discussion will include thoughts of creating things.
2. Teachers will read a brief nonfiction account of Benjamin Franklin or show a brief video. A good book for this would be the Barretta book. Students will be led in a discussion on who Franklin was. Teachers will write on the class display unit or board about Franklin's roles. Teachers will then help students inquire and curate information as they create a list of things that Franklin did and created, as seen in the teacher-read nonfiction book.
3. Since the worksheet shows Benjamin Franklin with a key and kite, teachers will spend time clarifying what Franklin's kite and key created. The Socratica Kids video explains that concept too.

4. Student groups will question, include and collaborate in the small group, find information, and explore and research by simply browsing detailed facts and illustrations in nonfiction sources to see if they could add more things to the class list of things that Franklin did.

5. The class will reflect and discuss a way that they and their neighborhood profit from Benjamin Franklin's ideas and creations. One thing that could be emphasized was that Franklin's inventions lead to the discovery of electricity and so electricity eventually made way for lights.

6. Teachers will list the first two worksheet answers on the board. Students will complete the rest of their worksheets themselves.

7. Students will share their worksheet answers.

Recommended Resources

Fiction

Anderson, Jessica L. *Brownies with Benjamin Franklin.* Vero Beach, FL: Rourke, 2016. [Just read parts of this.]

Breen, Steve. *Violet the Pilot.* Fort Collins, CO: Puffin, 2016.

Funk, Josh. *Albie Newton.* New York: Sterling, 2018.

Gail, Chris. *Awesome Dawson.* New York: Little, Brown and Company, 2013.

Jones, Pip. *Izzy Gizmo.* Atlanta, GA: Peachtree, 2018.

Long, Llana. *Ziggy's Big Idea.* Minneapolis, MN: Kar-Ben Publishing, 2014.

Rocsenstock, Barb. *Thomas Jefferson Builds a Library.* Honesdale, PA: Calkins Creek, 2013.

Spires, Ashley. *The Most Magnificent Thing.* Toronto, ON: Kids Can Press, 2014.

Sprio, Ruth. *Made by Maxine.* New York: Dial Books, 2018.

Nonfiction

Adler, David A. *A Picture Book of Benjamin Franklin.* New York: Holiday House, 2018.

Barretta, Gene. *Now & Ben: The Modern Inventions of Benjamin Franklin.* New York: Square Fish/Holt, 2009.

Bennett, Doraine. *Benjamin Franklin.* New York: AV2 by Weigl, 2019.

Dustman, Jeanne. *Benjamin Franklin: Thinker, Inventor, Leader.* Huntington Beach, CA: Teacher Created Materials, 2011.

Goldsworthy, Steve. *Benjamin Franklin.* New York: AV2 by Weigl, 2015.

Haldy, Emma E. *Benjamin Franklin.* Mankato, MN: Cherry Lake Publishing, 2017.

Keenan, Shelia. *Ben Franklin Thinks Big.* New York: HarperCollins, 2018.

Murphy, Frank. *Ben Franklin and the Magic Squares.* New York: Random House, 2001.

Nettleton, Pamela H. *Benjamin Franklin: Writer, Inventor, Statesman.* Mankato, MN: Picture Window Books, 2004.

Socratica Kids. "Benjamin Franklin for Kids—Ben Franklin Kite Experiment—Electricity for Kids." Video. Updated 2017. https://www.youtube.com/watch?v=rriVOlbw8Tg.

Strand, Jennifer. *Benjamin Franklin.* Mankato, MN: ABDO, 2017.

Will, Mara. *Benjamin Franklin.* Chicago, IL: Children's Press, 2015.

Land of the Free

List some ways that immigrants have helped your state or the United States:

Why do people from other countries want to live in your state or in the United States?

What countries do immigrants come from when they come to your state or country?

The people of the United States have immigrants in most all families and some from many years ago. What countries did your relatives come from many years ago or not too long ago?

Land of the Free, Directions

History: Immigration in basics and related to a state
Grade Levels Suggested: Third Grade or Third–Fifth Grades

Standards

AASL Standards

AASL Standards are listed at the start of each chapter, as each of those given standards are used in each lesson, as they are centered on students who "inquire, include, collaborate, curate, explore, and engage" (American Association of School Librarians 2017).

Common Core Language Arts Literacy Standards

CCSS.ELA-Literacy.RL.3.1 • Ask and answer questions to demonstrate understanding of a text, referring explicitly to the text as the basis for the answers.
CCSS.ELA-Literacy.RI.3.7 • Use the information gained from illustrations (e.g., maps and photographs) and the words in a text to demonstrate understanding of the text (e.g., where, when, why, and how key events occur).
CCSS.ELA.RL.4.2 • Determine a theme of a story, drama, or poem from details in the text; summarize the text.

Social Studies Standards C3

D2.His.3.3-5. Create questions of individuals and groups who made historical changes.
D2.His.16.3-5. Use evidence to create a claim about the past.

Learning Objectives

Students will

- Discuss the theme and main plot of an easy fiction book after hearing a story about an immigrant or immigration.
- Use information from illustrations and key words and research in small groups' basic immigration information.
- Create a folding booklet with immigration information.

Suggested Teaching Team

School library and social studies teachers.

Instructional Procedure

Lessons will be a collaborative student lesson for most of the class time. Students are more often than not involved in paired or team work so that all learners have a chance to gather ideas and be involved. Assessment is ongoing observation while also checking for understanding.

1. This lesson may require two sessions.
2. Theme and main plot will be discussed after teachers read a picture fiction book about immigrants or immigrations. Teachers will then ask students what country their ancestors came from and write that country name on the class board.
3. Teachers will ask if students know that the Statue of Liberty welcomes people to America. The statue symbolizes freedom. Teachers will briefly show pages of illustrations of the Statue of Liberty, as students glean two to three facts from illustrations and brief text.

4. Teachers will introduce the student worksheet by explaining that the United States is made up of people from many different countries. They will explain that immigrants have brought many talents to the country. Teachers will explain that people came to America for a reason.

5. Student groups will question, collaborate and include everyone within the group, curate (gather information while choosing a good source), and explore or read and answer the worksheet questions while using the listed Recommended Resources for states and other nonfiction information for the country.

6. Students will make a Statue of Liberty folding booklet. They will cut out the booklet in one big shape and fold the pages for the booklet. Students will need to decorate the cover and write a title on the cover, which could be "Land of the Free."

7. Students can write more information on the back pages of the booklet, perhaps including the data from the worksheet question.

Recommended Resources

Fiction

Danticut, Edwidge. *Mama's Nightingale: A Story of Immigration and Separation.* New York: Dial Books, 2015.

De Arias, Patricia. *Marwan's Journey.* Hong Kong: Minedition, 2018.

De La Pena, Matt. *Carmela Full of Wishes.* New York: G.P. Putnam's Sons, 2018.

Fox, Mem. *I'm an Immigrant Too!* San Diego, CA: Beach Lane Books, 2018.

Glaser, Linda. *Emma's Poem: The Voice of the Statue of Liberty.* New York: Houghton, Mifflin Harcourt, 2010.

Mils, Deborah. *La Frontera/The Border: El Viaje Con Papa/My Journey with Papa* [Bilingual]. Cambridge, MA: Barefoot Books, 2018.

Morales, Yuyl. *Dreamers.* New York: Neal Porter Books, 2018.

O'Brien, Anne S. *A Path of Stars.* Watertown, MA: Charlesbridge, 2012.

Ringgold, Faith. *We Came to America.* New York: Alfred A. Knopf, 2016.

Watts, Jeri. *A Piece of Home.* Somerville, MA: Candlewick, 2016.

Yaccarino, Dan. *All the Way to America: The Story of a Big Italian Family and a Big Shovel.* Edmond, OK: Dragonfly, 2014.

Yangsook, Choi. *Name Jar.* Edmond, OK: Dragonfly, 2003

Nonfiction

Bailey, R. J. *Statue of Liberty.* Minneapolis, MN: Jump!, 2017.

Bauer, Marion D. *The Statue of Liberty.* New York: Simon, 2019.

Brundle, Harriet. *Immigration.* Norfolk, UK: Book Life, 2016.

Coy, John. *Their Great Gift.* Minneapolis, MN: Carolrhoda, 2016.

Galka, Max. "Everyone Who's Immigrated to the U.S. since 1820." Updated 2016. http://metrocosm.com/animated-immigration-map/.

Hearn, Emily, and Marywinn Milne. *Our New Home: Immigrant Children Speak.* Toronto, ON: Second Story Press, 2009.

Herrington, Lisa M. *The Statue of Liberty.* Chicago, IL: Children's Press, 2014.

Housel, Debra J. *Famous Immigrants.* Huntington Beach, CA: Teachers Created Materials, 2008.

Kravitz, Danny. *Journey to America in the 1900s.* Minneapolis, MN: Capstone, 2015.

McArthur, Marcus. *Coming to America.* Huntington Beach, CA: Teacher Created Materials, 2013.

Metz, Lorigo. *A Nation of Immigrants.* New York: PowerKids Press, 2014.

Murray, Julie. *The Statue of Liberty.* Mankato, MN: ABDO, 2016.

Owens, Thomas S. *Immigrants and Neighbors.* Logan, IA: Perfection Learning, 2003.

Roberts, Ceri. *Refugees and Migrants.* New York: B.E.S. Publishing, 2017.

Scholastic. "Explore Immigration Data." Updated 2019. http://teacher.scholastic.com/activities/immigration/immigration_data/region.htm.

Scholastic. "Immigration Stories of Yesterday and Today" [Stories]. Updated 2019. http://teacher.scholastic.com/activities/immigration/young_immigrants.

Simms, Rose. *The Statue of Liberty*. Orlando, FL: Pop!, 2019.

Slingerland, Janet. *12 Immigrants Who Made American Sports Great*. Mankato, MN: 12-Story Library, 2019.

Terrell, Brandon. *12 Immigrants Who Made American Entertainment Great*. Mankato, MN: 12-Story Library, 2019.

Wallace, Sandra N. *First Generation: 36 Trailblazing Immigrants and Refugees Who Make America Great*. New York: Little, Brown and Company, 2018.

Nonfiction—Historical Immigration by State

Misra, Tanvi. "A State-by-State Map of Where Immigrants Came From." Updated 2015. https://www.citylab.com/life/2015/10/a-state-by-state-map-of-where-immigrants-came-from/408223/.

Vox. "160 Years of US Immigration Trends, Mapped." Updated 2015. https://www.vox.com/maps/2015/9/29/9408497/immigration.

Native Americans

1. There were many early famous Native Americans. One was Sequoyah, a Cherokee, who put his tribe's language into writing, which spread the tribe's history for all.

Write two facts on how the Cherokee tribe lived in the past: _____

_____

_____

2. A famous Native American group who helped in World War II were the Navajo code talkers. They helped by giving messages in a special code during the war. The code talkers were Navajo.

Write two facts on how the Navajo tribe lived in the past: _____

_____

_____

3. Now look up your state to see which Native American tribes lived in your state

in the past. Name one tribe: _____. Write how that

tribe lived in the past: _____

_____

_____

4. Colorfully design the Native American designs given above.

Native Americans, Directions

History: Native American Indians in the United States and in each U.S. state
Grade Levels Suggested: Third Grade or Third–Fifth Grades

Standards

AASL Standards

AASL Standards are listed at the start of each chapter, as each of those given standards are used in each lesson, as they are centered on students who "inquire, include, collaborate, curate, explore, and engage" (American Association of School Librarians 2017).

Common Core Language Arts Literacy Standards

CCSS.ElA-Literacy.RI.3.1 • Ask and answer questions to demonstrate understanding of a text, referring explicitly to the text for answers.
CCSS.ELA-Literacy.RI.3.7 • Use the information gained from illustrations (e.g., maps and photographs) and the words in a text to demonstrate understanding of the text (e.g., where, when, why, and how key events occur).

Social Studies Standards C3

D2.His.2.3-5. Compare life in certain history times to life today.
D2.His.3.3-5. Create questions on individuals and groups who made historical changes.
D2.His.16.3-5.Use evidence to create a claim about the past.

Learning Objectives

Students will

- Discuss a famous person and group of famous Native Americans in history.
- Use illustrations and text to research the Cherokee and Navajo tribal nations briefly.
- Locate key events to research the early Native American tribe found in their state.
- Color the Native American symbols.

Suggested Teaching Team

School library and social studies teachers.

Instructional Procedure

Lessons will be a collaborative student lesson for most of the class time. Teachers are always checking for understanding. Students are more often than not involved in paired or team work so that all learners have a chance to gather ideas and be involved. Assessment is ongoing observation while also checking for understanding.

1. Teachers will write on the class information board the following website for finding who the Native American tribes were in the students' state. Students will need that information for a worksheet question. The following internet site will give the names of early Native American tribes for each state and other tribal information: Native American Language of the Americas: http://www.native-languages.org/states.htm.

2. Teachers will briefly explain that Native Americans were the first inhabitants of the land that is now called the United States of America. Teachers will also show illustrations of Native American

famous people, such as Sequoyah and the Navajo code talkers. Using student worksheets, teachers will take a few seconds to read and explain why those two were famous.

3. Teachers will explain that students will find two facts on the early Cherokee and then two facts on the Navajo tribes before researching their own state's Native Americans.

4. Small groups will briefly question, include and collaborate with others in the group, and find information with text and illustrations in order to solve the worksheet questions. Teachers will guide the research by asking students to find facts on how the early tribal nations originally lived, got their food, or other such things.

5. Teachers will monitor the group work. As soon as small student groups have answered the first two worksheet questions, students will find out which Native American tribes were seen in their state in the past. They will use the previously given website to answer that worksheet question.

6. After finding out the early Native American tribes in their state, student groups will select one tribe, write down that name, and then find out two facts on how that tribe originally lived.

7. Students will briefly discuss how life has changed from the early Native American way in their state to how they see people live today.

8. Students will colorfully decorate the two Native American symbols located at the top of the worksheet. Students can use those two symbols as a decoration for their school lanyard if the two symbols are connected at the sides so that the lanyard can be strung through those symbols.

Recommended Resources

Nonfiction

Alchin, Linda. "Articles on the History of Native Americans." Updated 2017. https://www. warpaths2peacepipes.com/history-of-native-americans/.

Bodden, Valerie. *Cherokee*. Mankato, MN: Creative Education, 2018.

Britannica Kids. "Navajo Code Talkers." Updated 2019. https://kids.britannica.com/kids/article/ Navajo-code-talkers/601078/308251-toc.

Craats, Rennay. *The Cherokee*. New York: Weigl, 2016.

Craats, Rennay. *The Navajo*. New York: Weigl, 2017.

Cunningham, Kevin. *The Navajo. True Books*. Chicago, IL: Children's Press, 2011.

Kyle, Amarie. *Navajo*. New York: PowerKids Press, 2016.

Native American Language of the Americas. "Maps of the United States Indians by State." Updated 2014. http://www.native-languages.org/states.htm.

North American Indian Nations Set. [Indian nations by each major geographic U.S. area]. Minneapolis, MN: Lerner, 2017.

Peterson, Marie, ed. *Early American Indian Tribes: Early America (Social Studies Readers)*. Huntington Beach, CA: Teacher Created Materials, 2004.

Rodgers, Kelly. *Sequoyah and the Written Word*. Huntington Beach, CA: Teacher Created Materials, 2017.

Shaffer, Jody J. *What's Your Story, Sequoya?* Minneapolis, MN: Lerner, 2016.

Smith-Llera, Danielle. *The Cherokee: The Past and Present of a Proud Nation*. Minneapolis, MN: Capstone, 2016.

Spotlight on Native Americans [Book Set]. New York: PowerKids Press, 2016.

Strand, Jennifer. *Sequoyah*. Mankato, MN: ABDO, 2018.

TSI. "Navajo Americans. Navajo Tribe. Navajo Code Talkers." Updated 2018. https://www. ducksters.com/history/native_american_navajo.php.

Zardes, Cassandra. *Cherokee*. New York: PowerKids Press, 2015.

Great Inventors Changing America

Telegraph

Cotton Gin

1. Select and circle one of these great inventors: Thomas Edison, Alexander Graham Bell, Eli Whitney, or Samuel Morse. Pretend to be that inventor.
2. Use the picture. Change the picture to resemble your inventor, with a beard or other things.
3. Students will guess your inventor. Show your picture. Introduce yourself as an inventor; say something about your invention, another fact, and how the invention helped America.

Great Inventors Changing America

History: Inventors around the time of the Industrial Revolution and the changes on America
Grade Levels Suggested: Fourth Grade or Fourth–Fifth Grades

Standards

AASL Standards

AASL Standards are listed at the start of each chapter, as each of those given standards are used in each lesson, as they are centered on students who "inquire, include, collaborate, curate, explore, and engage" (American Association of School Librarians 2017).

Common Core Language Arts Literacy Standards

CCSS.ElA-Literacy.RI.4.1 • Refer to details and examples in a text when explaining what the text says explicitly and when drawing inferences from the text.

CCSS.ELA-Literacy.RI.4.7 • Interpret the information presented visually, orally, or quantitatively (e.g., in charts, graphs, diagrams, time lines, animations, or interactive elements on web pages), and explain how the information contributes to an understanding of the text in which it appears.

Social Studies Standards C3

D2.His.3.3-5. Create questions on individuals and groups who made historical changes.
D2.His.16.3-5.Use evidence to create a claim about the past.

Learning Objectives

Students will

- Discuss the main plot after hearing and seeing parts of a book or video about the Industrial Revolution.
- Select one of the four inventors and research that inventor in pairs.
- Use visual and textual information to find facts on a chosen inventor.
- Present their inventor in the form of a guessing game.

Instructional Procedure

Lessons will be a collaborative student lesson for most of the class time. Students are more often than not involved in paired or team work so that all learners have a chance to gather ideas and be involved. Assessment is ongoing observation while also checking for understanding.

1. Teachers will ask if the students know something that a famous inventor created. Then teachers will introduce the lesson by saying that some American inventors became famous around the time of the Industrial Revolution, which started in London, England. Teachers will show part of a video on the Industrial Revolution or skim and show just parts of a book on the Industrial Revolution.

2. Teachers will display the names of four American inventors for that time period: Samuel Morse, Thomas Edison, Eli Whitney, and Alexandra Graham Bell.

3. Student pairs will select, question and infer, collaborate, explore, and then research visual and textual nonfiction sources on one of those chosen inventors in order to gather information. Students will also modify the picture provided in the worksheet to best resemble their chosen inventor.

4. Engaged student pairs will present their research to others. To other pairs, student pairs will re-present their inventor without telling their inventor's name but will say what was invented and

another fact like any problems with the invention or with inventing and how the invention helped America. Other pairs will guess the identity of that inventor.

5. Teachers will ask students to summarize how the four inventors changed America.

Recommended Resources

Nonfiction

A&E Television Networks. "Biography.com." https://www.biography.com. [Can find all four inventors here].

Bader, Bonnie. *Who Was Alexander Graham Bell?* New York: Grossett & Dunlap, 2013.

Brasch, Nicolas. *The Industrial Revolution: Age of Invention.* New York: PowerKids Press, 2013.

Cefrey, Holly. *The Inventions of Eli Whitney: The Cotton Gin.* New York: PowerKids Press, 2003.

Davis, Lynn. *Alexander Graham Bell.* Mankato, MN: ABDO, 2016.

Davis, Lynn. *Samuel Morse.* Mankato, MN: ABDO, 2016.

Davis, Lynn. *Thomas Edison.* Mankato, MN: ABDO, 2016.

Garcia, Tracy J. *Eli Whitney* [Graphic Novel]. New York: PowerKids Press, 2013.

Garcia, Tracy J. *Thomas Edison.* New York: PowerKids Press, 2013.

Garsetecki, Julia. *Life during the Industrial Revolution.* Mankato, MN: ABDO, 2015.

Hamen, Susan. *America Enters the Industrial Revolution.* Vero Beach, FL: Rourke, 2013.

Happy Learning English. "Adventure into the Industrial Revolution." Updated 2018. https://www.youtube.com/watch?v=Xh_Lk7kDrUI.

James, Emily. *Alexander Graham Bell.* Mankato, MN: Capstone, 2017.

Kerby, Mona. *Samuel Morris.* Westminster, MD: MK, 2018.

Kreig, Katherine. *Thomas Edison: World Changing Inventor.* Mankato, MN: ABDO, 2014.

Lynch, Seth. *The Industrial Revolution.* Milwaukee, WI: Gareth Stevens, 2018.

Martin, Justin. *Easy Reader Biographies: Alexander Graham Bell: A Famous Inventor.* New York: Scholastic, 2007.

McDaniel, Melissa. *The Industrial Revolution.* New York: Scholastic, 2011.

Niver, Heather M. *Eli Whitney and the Industrial Revolution.* New York: PowerKids Press, 2016.

Royston, Angela. *Inventors Who Changed the World.* New York: Crabtree, 2010. [This source includes James Watt].

Schaefer, Lola M. *Alexander Graham Bell.* Mankato, MN: Capstone, 2016.

Seidman, David. *Samuel Morse and the Telegraph.* Mankato, MN: Capstone Press, 2007.

Spilsbury, Louise. *Alexander Graham Bell and the Telephone.* New York: PowerKids Press, 2016.

Stoltman, Joan. *20 Fun Facts about the Industrial Revolution.* Milwaukee, WI: Gareth Stevens, 2018.

Strand, Jennifer. *Thomas A. Edison.* Mankato, MN: ABDO, 2017.

TSI. "Biography." https://www.ducksters.com/biography. [One can find all four inventors here].

WORLD AHOY. "The Industrial Revolution." WORLD AHOY Animation Series Ep.18. Video. Updated 2016. https://www.youtube.com/watch?v=IeD7mYk_Wq0.

Women Have Rights

Vote!

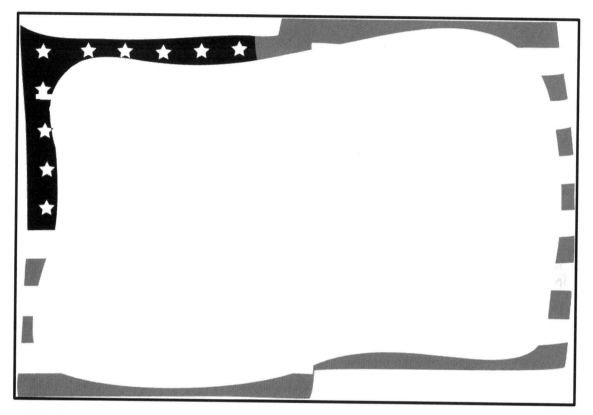

1. Elizabeth Cady Stanton and Susan B. Anthony worked to help women to be able to vote. Describe two things that these women did to help women with voting.

2. Why didn't women have the right to vote in elections?

Since Elizabeth Cady Stanton and Susan B. Anthony did rallies or marches to try to help women to vote, create a rally or march too! March for the right of women to vote!

3. Write three to four reasons about helping women to vote.

4. Create a sign! Colorfully write your message on the sign given earlier! Cut out your sign.

5. Now march with your sign and loudly repeat your reasons to help women to vote.

From *New Standards-Based Lessons for the Busy Elementary School Librarian: Social Studies* by Joyce Keeling. Santa Barbara, CA: Libraries Unlimited. Copyright © 2020.

Women Have Rights, Directions

History: History of women's right to vote
Grade Levels Suggested: Fourth Grade or Fourth–Five Grades

Standards

AASL Standards

AASL Standards are listed at the start of each chapter, as each of those given standards are used in each lesson, as they are centered on students who "inquire, include, collaborate, curate, explore, and engage" (American Association of School Librarians 2017).

Common Core Language Arts Literacy Standards

CCSS.ELA-Literacy.RL.4.1 • Refer to details and examples in a text when explaining what the text says explicitly and when drawing inferences from the text.
CCSS.ELA.RL.4.2 • Determine a theme of a story, drama, or poem from details in the text; summarize the text.
CCSS.ELA-Literacy.RI.4.7 • Interpret information presented visually, orally, or quantitatively (e.g., in charts, graphs, diagrams, timelines, animations, or interactive elements on web pages), and explain how the information contributes to an understanding of the text in which it appears.

Social Studies Standards C3

D2.His.3.3-5. Create questions of individuals and groups who made historical changes.
D2.His.16.3-5.Use evidence to create a claim about the past.

Learning Objectives

Students will

- Discuss the theme and main plot of a picture book after hearing the story or discussing a video on women's rights.
- Research and interpret visually and from text details on Elizabeth Cady Stanton and Susan B. Anthony and suffrage.
- Answer the questions given in their worksheets.
- Create a rally or march.
- Relate the Nineteenth Amendment to the lesson.

Suggested Teaching Team

School library and social studies teachers.

Instructional Procedure

Lessons will be a collaborative student lesson for most of the class time. Teachers are always checking for understanding. Students are more often than not involved in paired or team work so that all learners have a chance to gather ideas and be involved. Assessment is ongoing observation.

1. Teachers will ask why it is important to vote for things. Then they will mention that women could not vote for many years. The women's fight to vote was called women's suffrage.
2. Theme and main plot will be discussed after teachers read a picture fiction book about women's suffrage or show a video on the topic.

3. Students will brainstorm some ideas on why or why not women should be allowed to vote. The class will make a class list on the pros and cons of women's right to vote, as related to prior knowledge and reflections.

4. Teachers will explain that Elizabeth Cady Stanton and Susan B. Anthony helped to push the right to vote for women. Small student groups will be asked to question or inquire, collaborate, explore, and research using illustrations and text details about Stanton and Anthony.

5. Using the worksheet, small groups will discuss Stanton and Anthony. They will create a classroom rally or march by questioning, collaborating, and thinking of reasons for the women's right to vote; colorfully decorate the poster on the worksheet; cut out the poster; and actually march in the classroom! Each student will want to decorate a worksheet sign.

6. Small groups will march and loudly proclaim their reasons as well as show their signs.

7. Finally, teachers will ask students to answer which U.S. constitutional amendment finally gave women the privilege to vote after many years. The group that did the best rally or march will read the Nineteenth Amendment together.

8. If time permits, students can find more facts.

Recommended Resources

Fiction

Karr, Kathleen. *Mama Went to Jail for the Vote*. New York: Hyperion, 2005.

Murphy, Claire R. *Marching with Aunt Susan*. Atlanta, GA: Peachtree, 2017.

Robbins, Dean. *Miss Paul and the President. The Creative Campaign for Women's Right to Vote*. New York: Knopf, 2016.

Rockliff, Mara. *Around America to Win the Vote*. Somerville, MA: Candlewick, 2016.

White, Linda A. *I Could Do That! Esther Morris Gets Women the Vote*. New York: Farrar, Straus and Giroux, 2005.

Winter, Jonah. *Lillian's Right to Vote: A Celebration of the Voting Rights Acts of 1965*. New York: Schwartz & Wade, 2015.

Nonfiction

Benoit, Peter. *Women's Right to Vote*. Chicago, IL: Children's Press, 2014.

Carson, Mary K. *Why Couldn't Susan B. Anthony Vote and Other Good Questions about Women's Suffrage*. New York: Sterling, 2015.

Clay, Kathryn. *The U.S. Constitution: Introducing Primary Sources*. Minneapolis, MN: Capstone Press, 2016.

Connors, Kathleen. *The Life of Susan B. Anthony*. Milwaukee, WI: Gareth Stevens, 2014.

DreamWorksTV. "Susan B. Anthony: 'Vote! Vote! Vote!' " Video. Updated 2016. https://www.youtube.com/watch?v=vfyCgGdznv4.

Gillibrand, Kirsten. *Bold & Brave. Ten Heroes Who Won Women the Right to Vote*. New York: Alfred A. Knopf, 2018.

Harris, Duchess. *Women's Suffrage*. Mankato, MN: ABDO, 2018.

Isecke, Harriet. *Susan B. Anthony & Elizabeth Cady Stanton*. Huntington Beach, CA: Teacher Created Materials, 2012.

Kamma, Anne. *If You Lived When Women Won Their Rights*. New York: Scholastic, 2008.

Keppeler, Jill. *Women's Suffrage Movement*. New York: PowerKids Press, 2017.

Kids.Net.Au. "Nineteenth Amendment to the United States Constitution." http://encyclopedia.kids.net.au/page/ni/Nineteenth_Amendment_to_the_United_States_Constitution.

Kuligowski, Stephanie. *Susan B. Anthony*. Huntington Beach, CA: Teacher Created Materials, 2016.

Lonrijo, Metz. *The Women's Suffrage Movement*. New York: PowerKids Press, 2014.

Malaspina, Ann. *Heart on Fire: Susan B. Anthony Votes for President.* New York: AV2 by Weigl, 2015.

"19th Amendment." http://www.government-and-constitution.org/amendments/19th-amendment.htm.

Penne, Barbara. *Susan B. Anthony: Pioneering Leader of the Women's Rights Movement.* New York: Rosen, 2016.

Pollack, Pam. *Who Was Susan B. Anthony?* New York: Grosset & Dunlap, 2014.

Rappaport, Dorren. *Elizabeth Started All the Trouble.* New York: Hyperion, 2016.

Rice, Dona. *Susan B. Anthony.* Huntington Beach, CA: Teacher Created Materials, 2012.

Rossi, Ann. *Created Equal: Women Campaign for the Right to Vote, 1840–1920.* Washington, DC: National Geographic, 2005.

School House Rock. "Suffern Til Suffrage." Video. Updated 2012. https://www.youtube.com/watch?v=CGHGDO_b_q0.

Spiller, Sara. *Susan B. Anthony.* Mankato, MN: Cherry Lake Publishing, 2019.

Stoltman, Joan. *Elizabeth Cady Stanton.* Milwaukee, WI: Gareth Stevens, 2019.

Stone, Tanya L. *Elizabeth Leads the Way: Elizabeth Cady Stanton and the Right to Vote.* New York: Square Fish, 2010.

Travis, Cathy. *Constitution Translated for Kids.* Washington, DC: We the Books, 2016.

Tea Party

1. What was the Boston Tea Party?

2. What did the Boston Tea Party have to do with the American Revolution?

3. List two or three other taxes that colonial people did not like.

4. Debate! You will be chosen to be either a loyalist (loyal to Britain) or a patriot. Find two facts to back or defend being a loyalist or a patriot. Then debate being a loyalist or a patriot.

	Loyalist	Patriot
Fact #1		
Fact #2		

From *New Standards-Based Lessons for the Busy Elementary School Librarian: Social Studies* by Joyce Keeling. Santa Barbara, CA: Libraries Unlimited. Copyright © 2020.

Tea Party, Directions

History: Boston Tea Party changed the country
Grade Levels Suggested: Fifth Grade or Fourth–Fifth Grades

Standards

AASL Standards

AASL Standards are listed at the start of each chapter, as each of those given standards are used in each lesson, as they are centered on students who "inquire, include, collaborate, curate, explore, and engage" (American Association of School Librarians 2017).

Common Core Language Arts Literacy Standards

CCSS.ELA-Literacy.RI.5.7 • Draw on the information from multiple print or digital sources, demonstrating the ability to locate an answer to a question quickly or to solve a problem efficiently.

CCSS.ELA-Literacy.R.I.5.9 • Integrate the information from several texts on the same topic in order to write or speak about the subject knowledgeably.

Social Studies Standards C3

D2.His.16.3-5. Use evidence to create a claim about the past.

Learning Objectives

Students will

- Discuss the major events of the Boston Tea Party.
- Research the Boston Tea Party and colonial taxation.
- Research in small groups the loyalist or patriot views, and then debate that issue.

Suggested Teaching Team

School library and social studies teachers.

Instructional Procedure

Lessons will be a collaborative student lesson for most of the class time. Teachers are always checking for understanding. Students are more often than not involved in paired or team work so that all learners have a chance to gather ideas and be involved. Assessment is ongoing observation.

1. Teachers will briefly explain that the thirteen American colonies were under the rule of Great Britain. Things changed when the people had to pay taxes and could not say anything about that decision. Some colony people did not like the taxes and rules, and so they rebelled. Those people were called the patriots, and those who were loyal to the country of Britain were called loyalists (Tories). The loyalists liked having the security of belonging to the British because of their powerful navy and other considerations.

2. Teachers will show a video about the Boston Tea Party or read a book on that topic. Discussion will include the theme and events.

3. Small student groups of three or four students will question, collaborate, discuss, reflect, explore, read, and complete problem solving on the first three questions on the worksheet.

4. The class will then regroup. The entire class will be split by teachers into two groups of either the patriots or the loyalists. The patriot and the loyalist groups will be broken down into small groups

in order to create a debate or take a stance for their position. Students must have at least two strong facts and opinions based on logic or facts. Teachers will need to monitor students debate facts and ideas.

5. Student groups will debate against each other as assigned by teachers.

Recommended Resources

Nonfiction

Boston Tea Party Ships & Museum. "Boston Tea Party Facts." Video. Updated 2019. https://www.bostonteapartyship.com/boston-tea-party-facts.

Britannica. "Loyalist." Updated 2019. https://www.britannica.com/topic/loyalist.

Britannica Kids. "American Revolution Background." Updated 2019. https://kids.britannica.com/kids/article/American-Revolution/353711/252749-toc.

Cook, Peter. *You Wouldn't Want to Be at the Boston Tea Party.* New York: Scholastic, 2014.

Forest, Christopher. *The Rebellious Colonists and the Causes of the American Revolution.* Minneapolis, MN: Capstone, 2013.

Gillman, Sarah. *The Boston Tea Party.* Berkeley Heights, NJ: Enslow, 2016.

Gondosch, Linda. *How Did Tea and Taxes Spark a Revolution.* Minneapolis, MN: Lerner, 2010.

Harper, TeVon. "Grio B.—Party's Going On (Boston Tea Party Rap)." Video. Updated 2015. https://www.youtube.com/watch?v=LFq657QFNqc.

History.com, eds. "Boston Tea Party." Updated 2018. https://www.history.com/topics/american-revolution/boston-tea-party.

Hull, Mary E. *Witness the Boston Tea Party in United States History.* Berkeley Heights, NJ: Enlsow, 2015.

Krull, Kathleen. *What Was the Boston Tea Party?* New York: Penguin, 2013.

Liberty's Kids. "Season 01 Episode 01 the Boston Tea Party." Video. Updated 2015. https://www.youtube.com/channel/UC5pJi9mLIy38m2e_u3sboKQ.

MacCarald, Clara. *The American Revolution.* Mendota Heights, MN: Focus Readers, 2018.

Nassabaum. "Boston Tea Party Video." Video. https://www.mrnussbaum.com/history-2-2/boston-tea-party/.

Prior, Jennifer. *Reasons for a Revolution.* Huntington Beach, CA: Teacher Created Materials, 2017.

Sanderson, Whitney. *The Boston Tea Party Sparks Revolution.* Philadelphia, PA: Momentum, 2018.

Squadrin, Giulia. "Difference between Patriots and Loyalists. DifferenceBetween.Net." Updated 2018. http://www.differencebetween.net/miscellaneous/politics/difference-between-patriots-and-loyalists/.

Thornton, Jeremy. *Tories and Patriots Neighbors at War.* New York: PowerKids Press, 2003.

Tovar, Alicia. *The Boston Tea Party: No Taxation without Representation.* New York: PowerKids Press, 2015.

TSI. "American Revolution. Patriots and Loyalists." Updated 2019. https://www.ducksters.com/history/american_revolution/patriots_and_loyalists.php.

TSI. "Causes of the American Revolution." Updated 2010. https://www.ducksters.com/history/american_revolution/causes_revolutionary_war.php.

Webb, Robert N. *We Were There at the Boston Tea Party.* Mineola, NY: Dover, 2013.

Webb, Sarah P. *A Primary Source History of the American Revolution.* Minneapolis, MN: Capstone, 2016.

White, David. "Social Studies for Kids: Boston Tea Party." Updated 2019. http://www.socialstudiesforkids.com/articles/ushistory/bostonteaparty.htm.

Freedom

What do handcuffs and an ocean trade route have to do with freedom?

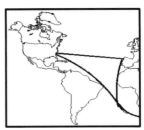

The slavery ocean route is shaped like a triangle or kite.

1. On a separate paper, create a list of two to three brief notes about each slavery topic: a reason for slavery, a slave's life, the Emancipation Proclamation, and the Thirteenth Amendment.

2. Then create a poem from your notes. Start each poem line with the letters listed.

Why slavery started in early America?

F_____

Life of a slave

R_____

Emancipation Proclamation

E_____

Thirteenth Amendment

E_____

3. Make a timeline. Draw a line from the preceding bold words to the time line year to show what happened in each approximate year.

| 1620 | 1660 | 1700 | 1720 | 1760 | 1800 | 1820 | 1860 |

Freedom, Directions

History: History of slavery in colonial and early America
Grade Levels Suggested: Fifth Grade or Fourth–Fifth Grades

Standards

AASL Standards

AASL Standards are listed at the start of each chapter, as each of those given standards are used in each lesson, as they are centered on students who "inquire, include, collaborate, curate, explore, and engage" (American Association of School Librarians 2017).

Common Core Language Arts Literacy Standards

CCSS.ELA-Literacy.RL.5.2 • Determine a theme of a story, drama, or poem from details in the text including how characters in a story or drama respond to challenges or how the speaker in a poem reflects upon a topic; summarize the text.

CCSS.ELA-Literacy.RI.5.7 • Draw on the information from multiple print or digital sources, demonstrating the ability to locate an answer to a question quickly or to solve a problem efficiently.

CCSS.ELA-Literacy.R.I.5.9 • Integrate the information from several texts on the same topic in order to write or speak about the subject knowledgeably.

Social Studies Standards C3

D2.His.2.3-5. Compare life in certain history times to life today.
D2.His.16.3-5. Use evidence to create a claim about the past.

Learning Objectives

Students will

- Discuss the theme and main plot of a picture fiction book after hearing the story or a video.
- Hear and discuss a poem.
- Research multiple resources and integrate that knowledge into notes on early American or colonial slavery.
- Create a short poem.

Suggested Teaching Team

School library and social studies teachers.

Instructional Procedure

Lessons will be a collaborative student lesson for most of the class time. Teachers are always checking for understanding. Students are more often than not involved in paired or team work so that all learners have a chance to gather ideas and be involved. Assessment is ongoing observation while also checking for understanding.

1. This lesson may require more than one library instructional visit.
2. Theme and main plot will be discussed after teachers read a picture fiction book or show part of a video about early American slavery. Teachers will then read a poem on slavery and ask students about their thoughts on that poem. Finally, teachers will point out the ocean route provided in the worksheet for getting slaves to the early American colonies.

3. Teachers will explain that students will research early American or colonial times' slavery. Using nonfiction sources, small student groups will question, include others in the group as they gather brief information, read, and find two or three facts on the first arrival of slaves from Africa, two or three facts about the life of slaves, a simple description of the Emancipation Proclamation, and a very simple Thirteenth Amendment description. Students will need to find an approximate year for each of these topics too.

4. Students will work in small groups for about five to seven minutes to find and quickly jot down quick facts and thoughts on the worksheet topics. The lesson is not meant to be comprehensive but to only gather an overview.

5. Using their worksheets, student pairs or small groups will write a brief list poem from the student-found facts by starting each line with the acronym letters of FREE.

6. Students will complete the timeline. They will draw a line from the guided words in bold print from the poem to the approximate year on the worksheet timeline. Students should use a combination of years for the date of a life of a slave after connecting lines for the rest of the topics.

7. After teachers have quickly checked for understanding, student groups will share their poems with the class.

Recommended Resources

Fiction

Bandy, Michael S., and Eric Stein. *Granddaddy's Turn.* Somerville, MA: Candlewick, 2015.

Grifalconi, Ann. *The Village That Vanished.* Fort Collins, CO: Puffin, 2004.

Hopkinson, Deborah. *Sweet Clara and the Freedom Quilt.* New York: Knopf, 2018.

Levine, Ellen. *Henry's Freedom Box: A True Story of the Underground Railroad.* New York: Scholastic, 2007.

Raven, Margot T. *Night Boat to Freedom.* New York: Square Fish, 2009.

Siegelson, Kim L., and Brian Pinkney. *In the Time of the Drums.* New York: Lee & Low books, 2016.

Nonfiction

Alexander, Richard. *The Transatlantic Slave Trade: The Forced Migration of Africans to America (1607–1830).* New York: PowerKids Press, 2016.

Baumann, Susan K. *The Middle Passage and the Revolt on the Amistad* [Graphic Novel]. New York: PowerKids Press, 2015.

Burgan, Michael. *African Americans in the Thirteen Colonies.* Chicago, IL: Children's Press, 2013.

Hall, Brianna. *Freedom from Slavery: Causes and Effects of the Emancipation Proclamation.* Minneapolis, MN: Capstone, 2014.

Hopper, Whitney. *Slavery in the United States: The "Abominable Trade."* New York: PowerKids Press, 2017.

Infoplease. "History of Slavery in America." https://www.infoplease.com/timelines/history-slavery-america.

Kamma, Anne. *If You Lived When There Was Slavery in America.* New York: Scholastic, 2014.

Keller, Kristin T. *The Slave Trade in Early America.* Minneapolis, MN: Capstone, 2016.

Liberty's Kids. "Liberty's Kids HD 138—Born Free and Equal. History Cartoons for Children." Video. Updated 2017. https://www.youtube.com/watch?v=SOTXIpvwzwU.

Linde, Barbara M. *Slavery in Early America.* Milwaukee, WI: Gareth Stevens, 2011.

Linde, Barbara M. *Slavery in North America.* Farmington Hills, MI: Lucent, 2017.

Lynch, Seth. *The Emancipation Proclamation.* Milwaukee, WI: Gareth Stevens, 2018.

MRD. "The Passage." Video. Updated 2013. https://www.youtube.com/watch?v=IDQSUvP9oxw.

National Geographic Society. "A History of Slavery in the United States." https://www .nationalgeographic.org/interactive/slavery-united-states/.

Ollhoff, Jim. *Years of Slavery*. Mankato, MN: ABDO, 2011.

Peterson, Marie. *Slavery in America*. Huntington Beach, CA: Teacher Created Materials, 2005.

Pratt, Mary K. *A Timeline History of the Thirteen Colonies*. Minneapolis, MN: Lerner, 2014.

Prentzas, G. S. *The Emancipation Proclamation*. Chicago, IL: Children's Press, 2011.

Rissman, Rebecca. *Slavery in the United States*. Mankato, MN: ABDO, 2015.

Sharp, Pearl S., and Virginia Schomp. *The Slave Trade and the Middle Passage*. New York: Cavendish Square, 2006.

Softschools.com. "Slavery. Slavery Timeline." http://www.softschools.com/timelines/slavery_ timeline/235/.

Steinkraus, Kyla. *Constitution*. Vero Beach, FL: Rourke Educational Media, 2014.

Thirteen Media with Impact: PBS. "Slavery and the Making of America." Updated 2004. https:// www.thirteen.org/wnet/slavery/timeline/1865.html.

Time Editors. *Our Nation's Documents: The Declaration of Independence, The Constitution, Gettysburg Address, Emancipation Proclamation, and More!* New York: Time for Kids, 2018.

Xina, M. *A Primary Source Investigation of Slavery*. New York: Rosen, 2019.

Nonfiction Poetry

Bryan, Ashley. *Freedom over Me: Eleven Slaves, Their Lives and Dreams Brought to Life*. New York: Atheneum, 2016.

Weatherford, Carole B. *Freedom on Congo Square*. New York: Simon & Schuster, 2016.

Bibliography

American Association of School Librarians. *AASL Standards Framework for Learners*. Chicago, IL: American Library Association, 2017.

Governors Association Center for Best Practices and Council of Chief State School Officers. *Common Core State Standards (Literacy)*. Washington, DC: National Governors Association Center for Best Practices and Council of Chief State School Officers, 2010.

National Council for the Social Studies. *Social Studies for the Next Generation: Purposes, Practices, and Implications of the College, Career, and Civic Life (C3) Framework for Social Studies State Standards*. Silver Spring, MD, 2013.

Nova. *Art Explosion 500,000*. Riverside, CA, 2010.

Index

167

About the Author

 JOYCE KEELING is the author of three other books to help elementary school librarians. She has taught elementary library classes and has been an elementary and a middle school library director for over twenty-five years. She holds a BA in elementary education, an MA in school library, and an education specialist degree in curriculum and teaching.